# Heroes
## of the
# Dawn

MYTH AND MANKIND

# Heroes
## of the
# Dawn

## CELTIC MYTH

BARNES
&NOBLE
BOOKS
NEW YORK

## MYTH AND MANKIND

**HEROES OF THE DAWN: Celtic Myth**

Writers: Fergus Fleming (Celtic World, Battles of the
Heroes, Tales of Magic, Legacy of the Celts)
Shahrukh Husain (Gods, Goddesses and the Cosmos)
C. Scott Littleton and Linda A. Malcor
(Legends of Arthur)
Consultant: Dr John McInnes

Created, edited and designed by
Duncan Baird Publishers
Castle House
75–76 Wells Street
London W1T 3QH

This edition published by Barnes & Noble, Inc.
by arrangement with Duncan Baird Publishers

2003 Barnes & Noble

ISBN 0-7607-3929-3

M 10 9 8 7 6 5 4 3 2 1

Colour separation by Colourscan, Singapore
Printed and bound by C S Graphics Shanghai

***Title page:*** **French 14th-century illuminated manuscript
of the *Histoire de Merlin* by Robert de Boron. The
scenes shown are part of the story of the grail.**

# Contents

# THE CELTIC WORLD

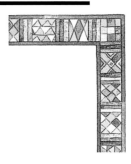

The fifty thousand Gauls in Alesia had no hope of escape. Around their besieged stronghold the Romans had dug two trenches, each five metres deep. Beyond these lay a field of iron barbs embedded in the ground, followed by a ring of camouflaged pits containing sharpened stakes. Then came a thicket of pointed branches. Next came a third trench, filled with water from a diverted stream. Beyond this was a four-metre-high rampart, bristling with more branches. And on top of the rampart stood a battlemented wooden palisade studded every eight metres with towers. Beyond the palisade lay more than one hundred thousand Roman troops. And beyond them – just in case the Gauls were hoping to be rescued – the same, mind-boggling array of fortifications was duplicated around a perimeter twenty kilometres in length.

*Below*: **Celtic warriors advance to the blast of the *carnyx* (war trumpet). From a 3rd-century BC cauldron found at Gundestrupp, Denmark.**

The whole siege system, erected in 50BC by some sixty thousand Roman legionaries over a period of only six weeks, showed just how seriously Julius Caesar took his enemy. And he had good reason for his precautions. For the Gauls were no mere mob of tribal malcontents. They were part of the Celtic nation, one of the great warrior peoples in European history. At its peak, only a few hundred years earlier, Celtic hegemony had extended over most of the European continent from Ireland and Iberia in the west through the Alps and the Balkans to Asia Minor in the east. In their time, Celtic warriors had cowed both Greek and Roman civilizations. By the first century BC, however, their power was on the wane. At the great siege of Alesia (modern Alise Sainte-Reine), which ended with the ignominious surrender of the Gaulish chieftain Vercingetorix, the Romans finally and uncompromisingly got their revenge for their own humiliating defeat by the Gauls more than three centuries earlier. The resistance of the Gauls was broken, and Alesia marked the end of the Celts' Continental supremacy. Although the Britons held out against Caesar, they too were to face defeat at the hands of his successors less than a hundred years later. Eventually, all Celtic regions except their remotest territorial outposts in the British Isles would fall under Roman sway. However, the ways and beliefs of the Celts, and above all their myths, would linger long after their material power had been extinguished.

*Opposite*: **Defiant and fearless in the face of defeat, a Celtic chief thrusts his sword into his own breast. A Classical sculpture of *c.*225BC.**

**CELTIC LANGUAGES**

Celtic speech was once heard throughout most of western Europe (see map below). Apart from names and a few short texts, not a great deal is known of Continental Celtic tongues, such as Gaulish, but what relics there are show a family likeness to surviving languages. The Gaulish *vindos* ("white" or "fair") corresponds to Irish *finn* and Welsh *gwyn*, for example, while *maros* ("big") becomes *mor* in Irish and *mawr* in Welsh. Modern Celtic tongues fall into two groups, "Goidelic" (Irish and Scottish Gaelic and the defunct Manx) and "Brythonic" (Welsh, Breton and the defunct Cornish). One of the most striking differences between the two groups is the occurrence of a k-sound in Goidelic for a p-sound in Brythonic: thus the words *ceann* ("head") and *mac* ("son") in Irish and Scottish Gaelic equate to Welsh *pen* and *ap*.

A Roman bronze statuette of a Celtic warrior in a horned helmet, *c.*250BC.

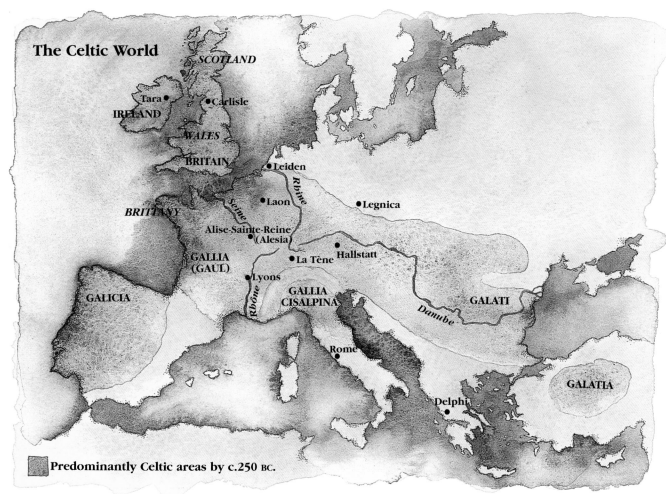

**The Celtic World**

SCOTLAND

Tara •   • Carlisle

IRELAND

WALES

BRITAIN

Leiden

Rhine

BRITTANY

Seine

Laon

Legnica

Alise-Sainte-Reine (Alesia)

La Tène   Hallstatt

GALLIA (GAUL)

Lyons

Rhône

GALLIA CISALPINA

GALATI

Danube

GALICIA

Rome

Delphi

GALATIA

Predominantly Celtic areas by c.250 BC.

## Warriors and Smiths

No one is quite sure when the Celts first emerged as a distinct culture. Linguistically, they belong to the Indo-European peoples, whose homeland was probably somewhere north of the Black Sea. Perhaps about seven thousand years ago, speakers of Indo-European dialects began to wander southwards towards India and westwards towards Europe. As the various groups of migrants moved further apart from one another, their speech diverged into a number of dialect groups that were the ancestors of most of the languages spoken in Europe and India today.

Speakers of what became the Celtic tongues appear to have arrived in the area of Germany's Harz mountains some time after 1000BC. The people they encountered there belonged to what is known as the "Urnfield" culture, so called after their cremation practices. As far as we can tell, the Urnfield people were a colourful group. They attached great importance to eating, drinking and fighting; they wore bright costumes; and they adorned themselves with a profusion of jewellery. Although there can be no certainty about it, the "Proto-Celtic" and Urnfield peoples seem to have combined, with the result that, perhaps *c*.800BC, the first distinctly "Celtic" culture was born.

These early Celts were skilled metalworkers. They introduced the art of iron-forging to Europe, and made innumerable agricultural advances – iron ploughshares, iron bridle bits, iron tyres for their carts, and even a form of iron reaper. They were accomplished warriors. The same technology that gave them ploughshares also provided them with swords, spears, arrows and, most awe-inspiring of all, iron-wheeled chariots.

Prosperous in peacetime, unstoppable in war, the Celts soon began to make their presence felt. By the sixth century bc they had expanded into what are now the Czech Republic, Slovakia and Austria, as well as Belgium, the Netherlands and all of northeastern France from Normandy to the Alps. Three centuries later they had occupied the rest of France, crossed the English Channel to Britain and Ireland, and occupied the western half of the Iberian peninsula. To the east, meanwhile, Celtic warriors had moved through the Balkans and established themselves in Galatia, in Asia Minor. The greatest civilizations of the time were powerless to stop the Celtic advance. In 387BC the emergent power of Rome received a shock when the Celts occupied the city in a seven-month orgy of looting and arson. The invaders left only after being struck by a debilitating epidemic – though not so debilitating, apparently, as to prevent them from extracting a massive payment from the Romans for the privilege of seeing them go. Almost a century later,

**Celtic graves at Hallstatt in Austria, excavated by the archaeologist Theodor Engel, 1846–63. His finds alerted Europeans to the sophistication of the ancient Celts.**

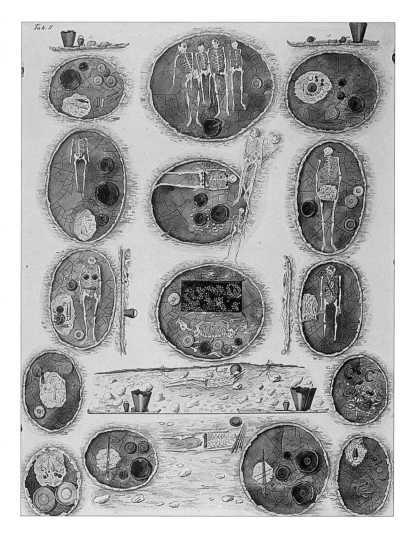

in 297BC, the Celts invaded Greece and sacked the sacred oracle town of Delphi, removing a large hoard of gold which eventually found its way to Toulouse. Even Alexander the Great found it prudent to concoct an alliance with the people whom the Greeks called *Keltoi* or *Galatai*.

The initial reaction to the Celts was fear. Outside Rome in 387BC, for example, the defenders "were frozen with fear by the appearance of the Gallic army and their tumult. They had innumerable horns and trumpets; and at the same time the whole army set up such a shouting that not only the instruments and the warriors but the hills around seemed to be raising their voices in echo." The Romans fled in terror without even giving battle.

In succeeding centuries, however, fear gradually gave way to curiosity. Present-day Celtic speakers are of various physical types. In ancient times, however, the differences between the Celts and their southern neighbours seem to have been very striking. Greeks and Romans described them as tall, fair and ruddy-complexioned. They bleached their hair with lime and drew it into spikes. Sometimes they dyed their skin blue. Their nobles grew long moustaches. When they went into battle nude – as they often did – they must have looked overpoweringly alien.

The Celts' love of fighting was another object of fascination. Whereas the Mediterraneans fought for a purpose, the Celts fought for the sake of it. If there was no obvious enemy within reach they would fight each other. One Roman writer described Celtic men as "terrible from the sternness of their eyes, very quarrelsome, and of great pride and insolence". Nor, to his dismay, did these qualities stop with the men. "A whole troop of foreigners would not be able to withstand a single one if he called to his assistance his wife, who is usually very strong." The Greek historian Strabo (64BC–

Circles, zigzags and geometric stylization were typical of early Celtic art, as on this pot of *c.*700BC, which was recovered from the river Loire in France.

AD21) was more blunt in his assessment. "The whole race," he concluded, "is war mad."

In battle they presented a terrifying spectacle, as recorded by Diodorus Siculus, a Roman historian of the first century BC: "They wear bronze helmets which possess large projecting figures that lend the wearer the appearance of enormous stature; in some cases there are horns on the helmet, while in other cases there are relief figures of foreparts of birds or beasts. Their trumpets ... produce a harsh sound which suits the tumult of war."

Their was a gaudiness, too, about the Celts, which the Mediterraneans found extraordinary. "To their frank and high-spirited character must be added a childish boastfulness and love of decoration," wrote Strabo. "They wear gold ornaments, torques on their necks and bracelets on their arms and wrists, while people of high standing wear dyed garments spangled with gold. This vanity makes them unbearable in victory." Diodorus Siculus commented on the Celts' fondness for striped cloaks "adorned with small, closely packed multi-coloured squares" – an ancestor of tartan.

The domestic life of the Celts reflected the same kind of exuberance. Sitting on furs, surrounded by spits and cauldrons from which they passed round hunks of roasted meat, they liked to eat and drink to excess. ("When they are eating," recorded one fascinated but fastidious Roman, "the moustache becomes entangled in the food, and when they are drinking, the drink passes, as it were, through a sort of strainer.") Both Greek and Roman observers noted that the Celts were very fond of alcohol and tended to become even more aggressive than usual under its influence. "At dinner they are liable to be moved by chance remarks to wordy disputes, and, after a challenge, to fight in single combat, regarding their lives as of no value."

From observations such as these the Mediterraneans had little hesitation in damning the Celts as uncivilized barbarians. Their judgment, however, was not impartial. In fact, the Celts were highly civilized. They were skilled farmers, miners and metal-workers. They possessed the administrative abilities to build and run wooden hilltop settlements of considerable size and sophistication. One, at Manching in south Germany, covered over four hundred and fifty hectares, and the six-kilometre wall that enclosed it was held together by two hundred and seventy tonnes of iron nails.

For most of the time, the Celts co-existed peacefully with their neighbours. They had a well developed trade network throughout Europe and the Mediterranean, and they exchanged commodities such as iron and salt – Celtic salted foods had a high reputation among Roman gourmets – for more luxurious fare such as wine and precious metals. Gaulish chiefs were fond of Greek goldware for their tables, as their graves attest.

It was not just material goods that flowed along the trade routes. There also came ideas. Designs originating in Italy, Greece, Persia and even India found their way into Celtic territories via the trade routes. Celtic artisans adopted the designs into their own repertoire and, in a short while, began to improvise upon them. From c.500BC, the trend blossomed into a new Celtic vernacular style known as "La Tène" from the Swiss site where artefacts in this style were first found in 1857. Classical art leaned towards order and symmetry, but La Tène reflected an imagination that drew deeply on the natural world. Its lines swooped and soared, whorled and looped, to create an image – or perhaps just the subtlest

The La Tène style reached its final flowering in Ireland in early medieval times. The astonishing skill of Irish craftsmen is seen to full effect in the so-called "Tara Brooch" of c.AD750.

hint of an image – of an animal, a branch of a tree, a human face. It was expressionistic, surreal at times, and always highly individual.

Underpinning this artistry was a belief system which was firmly rooted in nature. There is very little evidence that the Celts had an ordered hierarchy of gods equivalent to the Graeco-Roman pantheons. Their religious world was one of dream and superstition, magic and symbolism, through which roamed a plethora of unpredictable, shadowy deities. The Celts were closely in touch with the world about them and saw supernatural significance everywhere. To guide them through the numinous world around them they depended on the druids (see pages 39–41), who trained for two decades to learn by heart the huge quantities of Celtic spiritual lore. And therein lay the missing element in Celtic civilization: it had no written literature. "The druids," wrote Caesar, "believe that their religion forbids them to commit their teachings to writing." Possibly the druids feared that their wisdom would be corrupted and vulgarized if it was available to the masses in written form. However, the ban may partly have been for political reasons: written records would have greatly reduced the druids' prestige as the sole repositories of all religious and cultural knowledge.

The main result of this stipulation was that, before the Christian period, the Celts produced few written records of their beliefs – hence our reliance on the accounts of Classical writers for our knowledge of ancient Celtic myth. What we do have are mainly inscriptions. Anything on less durable material than stone and metal – and the Gauls did use writing for non-literary and non-religious purposes – has vanished without trace.

## The Decline of Celtic Power

The absence of written lore aside, there was no doubt that the Celts were a formidable civilization. They were never, however, a united one. There was no dominant Celtic people. At best they were a collection of tribes bound by a common language. And even that bond wore thin with time. By the second century bc an Irish Celt would probably have sounded strange, perhaps even incomprehensible, to a Celt from Britain or Gaul, let alone to those in Turkey, Italy and Spain (although as late as the fourth century ad one writer remarked that the Galatians – the Celts of what is now northern

Turkey – spoke a language that was almost the same as that spoken in a particular part of Gaul).

During the second and first centuries BC Roman civilization began to expand northwards into Gaul. The agent of expansion was often the well-armed and well-trained legionary. But just as often it was the adroitness of Roman diplomacy, reinforced by Roman coffers. It was a simple matter to offer one Celtic tribe support in its quarrels with another, and from there it was but a short step to offer paid employment in the fight against a supposedly common enemy. By the time a tribe realized its mistake, it was too late – its land had already

been subsumed within the empire. In 57bc, when Caesar claimed that most Gauls were Roman subjects, he was not exaggerating.

At this late stage the Gauls finally rallied to the common cause of liberty. But they had missed their chance. "I am a free man in a free state!" declared one chieftain. His stirring cry was echoed throughout Gaul. So, unfortunately, was his fate. Even as he spoke, Roman soldiers were cutting him down. The climax came with the fall of Alesia. "I did not undertake this war for private ends," announced Vercingetorix, the leader of the besieged, "but in the cause of national liberty." He then donned his finest robes and laid his arms at Caesar's feet. After six years of captivity, Vercingetorix was paraded like an animal before the Roman mob before being strangled.

**An early medieval mosaic of King Arthur from Otranto cathedral in southern Italy. The popularity of the Arthurian legends, with their strong Celtic elements, brought Europe into contact – unwittingly – with the ancient culture of the Celts.**

After the fall of Alesia, the Celts were finished as a force on the European mainland. And over the succeeding centuries the rest of their territories in the east and west went the way of Gaul. Only in the most outlying areas of the British Isles – Ireland, parts of Wales and the Highlands of Scotland – did independent Celtic communities survive. By the sixth century AD, however, even these regions had followed most of the rest of Europe in converting to a new culture altogether: Christianity.

And yet Celtic culture did not completely disappear. In fact, to a certain extent it found a new lease of life, as Christian scribes began to write down the old stories. For the first time, the gods and heroes of Celtic tradition emerged from the shadows. The Celtic spirit, immortalized in figures such as Finn, Cuchulainn and King Arthur, lived on.

# Celts, Romans and Christians

*Despite being Europe's dominant civilization for almost half a millennium, the Celts left little in writing to describe their world. What records survive have all been subjected to one form of censorship or another.*

Roman reports on Celtic civilization were produced mostly during Rome's imperial expansion and are infused with propaganda. Thus, Caesar praises the Gauls only when he is about to defeat them. Elsewhere, the Romans condemn cultural differences

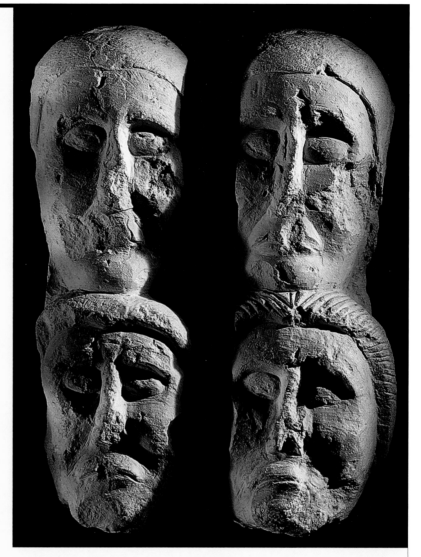

A 10th-century cross at Monasterboice, County Louth. The shape of the Celtic Christian cross derives from a pagan sun symbol, while the decoration belongs to the La Tène tradition.

out of hand as "barbarism". When the druids vanished so did centuries of accumulated oral wisdom, and what survives of pagan Celtic thought is embedded in the literature of Ireland, Scotland and Wales. But even here there are problems. The mythology was transcribed by Christian monks, who gave their own gloss to events. They replaced Celtic creation myths with the Book of Genesis, so we do not know how pagan Celts viewed the origin of the cosmos. In the monastic accounts, pagan myth and Christian history are

The Romans claimed that the Celts kept their enemies' heads as trophies. This may be true, since stone severed heads, such as these of *c.*200BC from southern France, adorned several monuments.

often intertwined. Thus the warrior Oisin returned from the pagan Otherworld to meet St Patrick, and myths of the goddess Brigit were absorbed into the legends of her Christian successor, St Brigit. The work of the monks is undoubtedly valuable, but it illuminates only from a distance the full glory of Celtic mythology.

*Right*: This 6th-century BC pendant brooch from a tomb at Hallstatt, Austria, bears circular emblems thought to be symbols of the sun. The upper part of the brooch resembles a boat, suggesting a link with the Otherworld (see page 28) where, later myths record, people went after death: it was often said to lie across water. At the top of the brooch are two stylized birds, creatures also linked with the Otherworld.
*Below*: Typical geometrical symbols and patterns of this era (c.800–c.500BC), which is called the Hallstatt period.

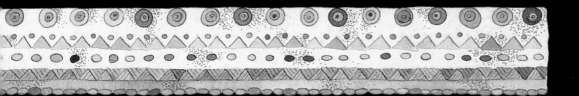

# ART, MYTH AND SYMBOL

The period before the great flowering of Irish literature yields few written sources for Celtic mythology other than those produced by the Romans. For the most part, we have to rely on scattered inscriptions on statues and coins. But clues also lie in the great array of brooches, horse-trappings, weaponry and other objects created by skilled Celtic artisans. These apparently silent witnesses are often adorned with characteristic motifs that at first sight appear to be purely decorative. However, the motifs can be shown to possess a profound symbolism that intimately reflects the spiritual culture in which the artists lived and worked.

*Above*: This decoration for a cup from Germany *c.*450BC combines Hallstatt sun symbols with plant motifs inspired by Mediterranean contacts. Plant and three-pointed triskele motifs (left) of this period (the early La Tène, *c.*500–*c.*300BC) reflect beliefs in the spirituality of nature and potency of threes.
*Right and above right*: An early La Tène brooch from Austria, and other designs based on the symbolic circle and drawn with compasses.

From the 4th century BC, plant and animal motifs became less naturalistic and more fluid, as the sample patterns (right) and bronze shields (below) illustrate. This reflects the Celtic mythic imagination, in which the real and fantastic were interwoven.

*Opposite*: The last flowering of the La Tène style is seen in the work of Irish book artists. This page of the Book of Kells (*c*.800AD) uses old motifs – circles, whorls, triskeles and fantastic beasts – to glorify Christ instead of the old gods.

Retrieved from the River Thames in London, this early 1st-century AD shield (above) bears a swastika-like wheel motif picked out in red enamel. This represents the later development of the circular sun-and-life symbol of the Hallstatt age, and it may have been intended to protect the bearer – although the shield was probably made not for combat but as a votive offering to river gods. The same purpose was no doubt served by the shield of c.150BC (detail, right) found in the River Witham in Lincolnshire. The stylized animal head may have been a mark of the bearer's status.

generatio

*Right*: Unbroken interlace patterns such as this could cover entire pages of Celtic illuminated manuscripts.

# GODS, GODDESSES AND THE COSMOS

A clap of thunder, a flash of lightning, a sudden downpour: these were sufficient signs to the ancient Celts that their gods were displeased. Celtic deities oversaw every aspect of the natural and supernatural worlds: thus Belenus, a sun god, fought with the storm god Taranis, "the Thunderer", to ensure that day followed night and that spring chased away the dark, barren winter. The Celts were a warrior people and worshipped an array of martial gods and goddesses. Some of the fiercest of these were female, such as the Irish goddess called the Morrigan. The British queen Boudicca or Boadicea invoked Andraste, a goddess of victory, when she sacked Roman Colchester, London and St Albans in AD60. War goddesses spurred warriors on to victory, but also appeared in the form of a raven or crow, an omen of death in battle.

Deities were often thought to live in old tombs like this one at Kilcooley in Donegal. Such tombs were also said to be entrances to the Celtic Otherworld.

Over all the gods and goddesses was an ancestral deity called simply "God" or "Father": an example is the Dagda, the "Good Father" of Irish myth. The Romans called one such deity by the name of their own god "Dis Pater" ("God Father"). Caesar used Roman names when he reported on Celtic gods, seeing them as local manifestations of Roman deities. The most popular god of the Gauls, he said, was

"Mercury", revered as "the inventor of all the arts". He was probably referring to Lugus, a god who gave his name to Lyon, Leiden and Carlisle and was no doubt related to Lugh, a divine warrior-craftsman of Irish myth.

The shared Indo-European origins of the Celts and Romans meant that both peoples had similar ancient myths about gods, heroes and the forces of nature. This common heritage may explain why the stories of a legendary Celtic ruler, Arthur, became so popular throughout medieval Europe: underlying many of the christianized tales of chivalry are ancient pagan themes of fertility and reverence for the land.

*Opposite*: The antlered fertility god Cernunnos was one of the most widespread Celtic deities. Here he is depicted on a 3rd-century BC cauldron found at Gundestrupp in Denmark.

19

# The Sacred World of the Celts

From inscriptions and written texts we know the names of about four hundred Celtic gods and goddesses. Probably three-quarters of these were local deities: there does not appear to have been a pantheon universally recognized throughout the Celtic world, akin to the Olympian gods of the Greeks and Romans. Those deities who were widely worshipped were often referred to by simple titles – Dagda ("Good God"), Matrona ("Mother"), Maponus ("Son" or "Youth"). Caesar said that the Gauls all claimed descent from a common divine ancestor whom they called simply "Father". For the most part, however, the divinities of the Celts were *genii loci*, "spirits of place", associated with a particular location.

This detail of a bronze votive wagon of *c.*650BC from southern Austria shows the stylized figure of a female deity, who supports what may be an incense burner. She is surrounded by mounted and dismounted male figures and two stags. The wagon, which stands 30cm high and 48cm long, may have been used for some ritual associated with hunting.

It is small wonder that Caesar observed that "the whole nation of the Gauls is greatly devoted to religious observances": wherever they went, the Celts were likely to enter on the terrain of a god, goddess or spirit, to whom due respect had to be paid. Before the coming of the Romans, however, it was unusual for the Celts to build permanent shrines to their deities: if a god or goddess was to be appeased or appealed to for help in some matter, the necessary rituals would have taken place in the open air at the sacred spring, grove, tree, waterfall or other feature that was associated with the relevant deity. It was only after the Roman conquests that temples were constructed over such sacred sites as the springs at Nemausus (Nîmes) in France and Aquae Sulis (Bath) in England.

Nor, on the whole, did the ancient Celts make images of their gods. Although early stylized figures occur, the idea of representing deities in realistic human form was another import from the Classical world. Just two centuries before the Roman conquest of Gaul, in 279BC, the Galatian leader Brennus mocked the human-like statues of the Olympian gods and goddesses that he saw during a Celtic invasion of Greece, indicating that the concept was clearly completely alien to the Celts. The idea must have become less strange, however, with the increasing contacts between the Classical and Celtic civilizations in the following centuries.

Some ancient Celtic deities may have taken the form of animals, later to become figures such as Cernunnos, the "Horned God", a widespread fertility god associated with forests, who was probably venerated as a "Lord of Animals". Cernunnos came to be depicted as a mature bearded man with antlers or horns. Other deities with close animal connections include the goddess Epona, who was associated with horses (see page 24), and the Morrigan, an Irish war goddess who could take the form of a crow (see page 25). In Celtic myth there are countless instances of transformation into animal form and back. Clearly, animals and birds were often believed to possess supernatural powers.

From Irish and Welsh writings we have some idea of the myths associated with the Celtic gods and goddesses as they were worshipped in the British Isles. However, as far as the Gauls and other continental Celts are concerned, the mythological record is patchy to say the least. Apart from votive monuments and a few coins, virtually the only clues are found on a single object: a silver cauldron found in 1891 at Gundestrupp in Denmark and dated to about 250BC. Although the cauldron ended up in Denmark it was probably made in southeastern Europe by Celts who, to judge from stylistic features, had contacts with Thrace and, through there, with Greece. The

Gods such as Lugus and Lugh were associated with light and may originally have been sun gods. The Celtic solar cult was part of a widespread ancient tradition, as seen in this votive wagon of *c.*1300BC depicting the sun drawn by a horse, which was found in Denmark.

# Roman and Celtic gods

The god Cernunnos flanked by the Roman gods Apollo (left) and Mercury; from a Gallo-Roman relief found at Rheims in France.

The Romans believed that most nations worshipped the same deities, although the names of the various gods and goddesses differed from land to land, and their functions also varied slightly according to local conditions. When Julius Caesar listed the most popular Gaulish deities in his *Gallic War,* he naturally gave them what he assumed to be their corresponding Roman names: Mercury, Apollo, Mars, Jupiter and Minerva. It is believed that "Mercury" refers to a god called Lugus. His cult centre, Lugdunum ("Fort of Lugus"), became the capital of Roman Gaul, and his festival, August 1, was chosen as the feast of Augustus,

the most important Roman holiday in Gaul. Many local gods were also identified with Mercury and became known by both their Roman and Celtic names, such as Mercury Artaios and Mercury Moccus. Likewise with Mars, who was not just a war god but also a guardian and healer: he was identified, for example, with Nodens, a healing god of southwest England. Another British healing deity, the goddess Sulis, was identified with Minerva and known as Sulis Minerva. Such divinities generally remained unmistakably Celtic, as seen in their distinctive dress, torques and weapons.

# The Great Hag

**In Irish and Scottish myth, features of the landscape were often said to owe their existence to a land goddess, the Cailleach Bheur, who took the form of a giant hag.**

Every night, after tending her cattle, the Great Hag went to the top of Ben Cruachan to block the spring that arose there with a huge boulder, so that it would not flood the plain below overnight. But one evening she fell asleep on her way up the mountain, and awoke to find the waters of the spring gushing out in a great torrent and cascading down the mountainside. In vain the Hag struggled to block the spring with the rock, but the force of the flood was too great even for her. Finally defeated, she looked down at the flooded valley and saw people and animals, dead and dying, in the floodwaters. She was so overcome with guilt that she turned into stone. The flooded plain became Loch Awe in Argyll.

*Left*: **A standing stone at Rossnowlagh in County Donegal, Ireland. Many such solitary stones were once worshipped as manifestations of the Great Hag.**

panels that make up the cauldron depict scenes and divinities with parallels in other sources: the Horned God is there, sitting among animals, and there is a bull hunt and a scene that shows a giant tipping warriors into a cauldron. These and other scenes recall such myths as the Irish *Cattle Raid of Cooley* (see pages 56–62) and the Welsh story of Bran the Blessed and the cauldron of rebirth (see pages 83–84), both recorded over a thousand years after the Gundestrupp cauldron was made.

## Sacred Numbers

Numbers played an important part in Celtic mystical thinking. The number five represented the world – north, south, east, west, and centre, as reflected, for example, in the five provinces of Ireland (see page 50). But the number three was paramount. The mystical quality of three was reflected in the three tiers of the universe – heaven, earth and Other-world, or sky, earth and sea – and the three types of being who inhabited the cosmos – mortals, deities and the dead. Celtic society, too, seems to have had three main strata: warrior-aristocrats, druids and craftsmen (who included bards and farmers). The festival of Samhain (October 31–November 1), which was a time when the frontier that normally separated the supernatural and natural worlds temporarily disappeared, was celebrated on the "Three Nights of Samhain".

Numerous Celtic deities possessed three manifestations, and images of such triple beings have been found all over the Celtic world. Among them are the *Genii Cucullati* ("Hooded Spirits"), fertility spirits which are depicted wearing long hooded capes. They are often found in the company of the triple mother goddess (see page 25). The triplication frequently implies great potency – very literally in the case of one statue of a Gaulish god, identified with the Roman Mercury, who is depicted with three phalluses. Many images of three-headed gods and animals also occur, and

Gaulish depictions of triple-horned bulls have been discovered by the dozen in many parts of France.

One of the most important Celtic concepts was the trinity of king, sovereignty and the land. Sovereignty was often personified as a powerful female deity, such as Queen Maeve of Connacht (page 58), who was probably a fertility goddess in origin. She is sometimes said to have been the lover of three times three kings.

In the myths, unusual phenomena tend to come in threes. The *Mabinogion* relates how, in the time of King Lludd, Britain suffered from three plagues, and the same work also refers to the

"Three Happy Concealments", "Three Unhappy Disclosures" and the "Three Men Who Broke Their Hearts With Worrying".

Multiples of three were also of significance to the Celts. There is some evidence that the Celtic month consisted basically of three weeks of nine days each plus feast days. The Fianna, Ireland's élite warrior band (see pages 62–68), was made up of platoons of twenty-seven men, and the voyager Mael Duin was warned by a druid that he must carry a crew of no more than eighteen including himself. When this number was exceeded, Mael Duin's ship was carried off into the Otherworld.

# The Mother Goddess

Among the most widely revered of Celtic deities were a range of powerful female figures who embodied the earth, fertility, fruitfulness and well-being. Shrines, statues and inscriptions to these mother goddesses have been discovered all over the Celtic world. They play an important role in Irish and Welsh mythology.

As a deity of fertility, the mother goddess was associated with promiscuous sexual activity – graphically seen in this pagan figure illustrating lust on a Norman church at Kilpeck in Herefordshire. She is known in Ireland as the Sheela na Gig.

In an age when most people did not live beyond early childhood, and when those who did spent most of their short lives in a constant struggle to avoid hunger and disease, the mother goddess was of central importance. She presided over all aspects of female fertility and childbirth, and was frequently depicted breastfeeding a baby. People appealed to her when they were pregnant or sick, and sometimes buried her image with the dead: one small statue of a mother goddess was found, poignantly, in the grave of a baby at Arrington in Cambridgeshire. Mother goddesses were also linked with the fertility of the land and individual prosperity, and could be shown dispensing apples, grapes, bread or coins to symbolize wealth and nature's bounty.

The Tuatha De Danann ("Children of the Goddess Danu"), the divine race of Irish myth, were said to be descended from one such goddess, Danu, who is probably identical to Anu, a goddess associated with the fertility of Ireland. Two round hills in County Kerry were once believed to be her breasts, reflecting her function as a divine mother; the hills are known to this day as "The Paps of Anu". She has a counterpart in the Welsh goddess Don, the divine matriarch of the *Mabinogion*.

Danu and Don are very much in the background of the myths, but other goddesses are more active. The Irish stories in particular feature a number of formidable divine matriarchs who embody the sovereignty and prosperity of the land. According to ancient tradition, the fertility of the soil and, therefore, the well-being of the people were only assured if the king coupled with one of these divinities. In pre-Christian times, the High King of Ireland was ceremonially "married" to a mother goddess as part of his inauguration ritual at Tara. This tradition is strongly represented in the myths: Queen Maeve, for example, who represented the sovereignty of Connacht, was said to have married nine successive kings of Ireland. *The Book of Invasions* recounts that when the Milesians, the ancestors of the Gaels, first came to Ireland, it was ruled by three kings, whose consorts were the divine matriarchs Eriu, Banbha and Fodla. The Milesians named the land after Eriu *(modern Irish Eire)* in return for a pledge that they and their descendants would always govern the island. It was

A votive sculpture of a triple goddess from Burgundy in eastern France. This particular goddess was especially popular in the region. The three female figures are holding things that clearly associate the goddess with motherhood: a baby, a cloth that may be a napkin, and sponges for washing. Each of the goddesses has one breast bared for suckling.

A drawing of Epona, after a monument to the goddess found in France. She was often shown carrying a large key, which has been interpreted as a symbol of her ability to unlock the gateway to the Otherworld. This recalls stories such as the Irish tale of the fairy woman Niamh, who entered the Otherworld on horseback with the hero Oisin (see page 30).

# Epona

**The ancient Celtic goddess Epona was linked with horses and motherhood, and is no doubt connected with the Welsh goddess Rhiannon and the Irish Macha.**

Dedications to Epona, whose name derives from the Celtic for "horse", have been found all over the former Celtic world. The goddess was usually depicted with horses or ponies, often mounted on a mare and dispensing fruit, grain or bread. She was especially popular in Burgundy, a centre of horse-breeding and home to the only known sanctuary dedicated to the goddess. Epona was sometimes portrayed as a triple mother goddess.

All riders – whether warriors, heroes, or just ordinary travellers – revered Epona. Roman cavalrymen worshipped her, and she was the only Celtic deity to be honoured with a festival at Rome, which took place on December 18. Epona's patronage of journeys had a profoundly spiritual aspect: she was connected with the journey of the soul from life to the Otherworld.

said that when a king was ritually married to Eriu, the goddess handed him a golden cup filled with red wine as a symbol of the sun and its benefits: the continued fruitfulness of the kingdom.

Other, even more formidable, Irish mother goddesses are closely associated with sexual potency, war and death. The most prominent of these is the Morrigan, who is said to have coupled with the Dagda, the tribal patriarch of the Tuatha De Danann. She also attempted to seduce the hero Cuchulainn, becoming his implacable foe when he

goddesses known as the Suleviae and associated with healing was worshipped as far apart as Hungary and Britain, where there were shrines at Cirencester, Colchester and Bath. Like images of individual goddesses, representations of the triple goddesses often show them bearing objects that symbolize motherhood or fertility, such as a baby, loaves or fruit. The triple goddess frequently appears alongside representations of the male triple god of fertility known to the Romans as the *Genius Cucullatus* or Hooded Spirit.

The central figure in this panel of the Gundestrupp cauldron is probably a mother goddess, perhaps one linked with war: a crow or raven perches on her hand and a fallen male lies at bottom right. The two smaller female figures may be aspects of the same deity.

rejected her advances. The Morrigan decided the fate of warriors, determining who would die in battle. Other deities representing this darker side of the mother goddess include Badb and Macha, and Maeve also has much in common with such figures. Both Badb and the Morrigan were able to metamorphose into a crow or raven, in which form they were said to hover over battlefields as harbingers of death to those fighting below.

Celtic mother goddesses are very commonly shown in groups of three, which the Romans called *Matres* ("Mothers") or *Matronae* ("Matrons"). Each of the figures in the triad represented a different aspect of the goddess, such as youth, maturity and old age, or birth, life and death. A trio of mother

The Second Branch of the *Mabinogion* is titled "Branwen, daughter of Llyr", although her role is less active than that of her brother Bran the Blessed. She is described in the story as one of the "three matriarchs of Britain", which may be a reference to an old triple goddess of sovereignty. This may also be where the twelfth-century writer Geoffrey of Monmouth got the idea that the mythical King Leir of Britain, who is derived from Llyr, had three daughters. In Ireland, the goddess Brigit was sometimes said to have two sisters of the same name – in origin the three Brigits were probably different aspects of one goddess. Irish war goddesses, such as Badb and the Morrigan, also sometimes appeared in the form of triple goddesses.

# Lords of the Heavens

The heavens played a central role in Celtic belief. They were the source of storms, alarming manifestations of divine power which also brought nourishing rain. Above all, the heavens were the domain of the sun, source of heat, light and growth. Several divine figures are closely linked with solar symbolism, such as Lugus, who is believed to be related to the Irish hero Lugh and the Welsh Lleu – all three names mean "Bright" or "Shining". Although Lugus may have been a sun god in origin, the Romans identified him not with Apollo, their god of light, but with Mercury.

A bronze Gallo-Roman statuette of the Hammer God from southeastern France. The style of the figure shows the extent of Roman artistic influence in this part of Gaul.

Apollo, on the other hand, was quickly associated with a popular Celtic deity called Belenus. One of Apollo's most important titles, Phoebus, means exactly the same as Belenus – "Brilliant" or "Bright" – and the Celtic god seems to have been allotted much the same range of functions as the Roman deity. Belenus was the lord of the sun, light and warmth, and may well have been the god who presided over the Celtic festival of Beltane (May 1), which celebrated the coming of summer. Like Apollo, Belenus was appealed to in times of sickness, reflecting the pervasive belief in the healing and sustaining powers of the sun.

Lugh and Lleu are not the only mythological heroes with solar connections. In Irish myth, Lugh is sometimes said to be the father of the Ulster hero Cuchulainn, whose hair was said to glitter "like the shining of yellow gold". At one point in *The Cattle Raid of Cooley*, he radiates so much heat that he melts the snow for ten metres all around him. Gawain, perhaps the most distinctly Celtic of the Arthurian heroes, was clearly linked to sun symbolism: his strength was said to increase as the sun grew stronger, reaching its peak at midday, and then to decrease as the sun went down. Cuchulainn and Gawain are involved in many similar adventures – Cuchulainn, for example, appears in a beheading episode very like the tale of Gawain and the Green Knight – and one theory claims that the two heroes have a common origin, perhaps as a tribal sun-hero of northwestern Britain.

Many Celtic gods were assimilated to Jupiter, the supreme lord of the heavens and the head of the Roman pantheon. As the ruler of high places, Jupiter was sometimes connected with local mountain deities, such as the Celtic Alpine gods Uxellinus and Poeninus. But most often he was identified with Celtic sky gods. Some of the most striking images of Jupiter from the Celtic world are monumental columns upon which the deity is portrayed as a mounted Celtic god of the skies. Many remains of such columns survive, mainly in eastern France and the Rhineland, and they usually depict the sky god vanquishing a giant beneath the hooves of his horse. This scene has been said to symbolize the eternal battle between the forces of prosperity and

Another widespread deity associated with the weather was the Hammer God, who is always shown carrying a pot and a big double-headed hammer with a long handle. He is called Sucellus ("Good Striker") in one inscription, although this may be a description rather than the god's name. Lyon, the focus of the cult of Lugus, was also an important centre for the worship of the Hammer God, which may suggest an affinity between the two deities. The Hammer God was sometimes depicted with sun symbols and was particularly popular in wine-growing regions. According to one theory, the god was believed to strike the hard

A cauldron was an attribute of the Dagda, and many similar vessels feature in Celtic myth. This wheeled cauldron of c.800BC, found in Romania, is adorned with stylized birds and was probably for ritual use.

light, represented by the sky god, and those of darkness and death, represented by the giant.

The sky god often bears a wheel, one of the commonest Celtic symbols of the sun, and a thunderbolt, representing the sky god's role as a god of storms. The thunderbolt was also the chief weapon of Jupiter, and he was sometimes specifically linked with Taranis, a Celtic storm god whose name means literally "Thunderer". Taranis appears to have been a widespread deity, although little is known of his cult. He may have been simply a divine personification of thunder, or he could have had a wider role as a bringer of rain and therefore of fertility.

frozen soil at the end of winter, heralding the return of the warm sun and making the earth soft for cultivation once more.

The Hammer God may be connected with the Dagda, the patriarch of the divine race of the Tuatha De Danann in Irish myth. The Dagda's attributes were similar to the hammer and pot: he carried a large club, with which he could both kill people and revive them, and a cauldron from which he dispensed a never-ending supply of food. Both gods possessed the power to overcome death, and the Dagda was said to wear a very short tunic, a characteristic garment of the Hammer God.

# The Otherworld

"It is the most delightful land of all that are under the sun; the trees are stooping down with fruit and with leaves and with blossom. Honey and wine are plentiful there; no wasting will come upon you with the wasting away of time; you will never see death or lessening. You will get feasts, playing and drinking; you will get sweet music on the strings; you will get silver and gold and many jewels. You will get everything I have said ... and gifts beyond them which I have no leave to tell of." Thus it was that the fairy-woman Niamh of the Golden Hair described to the warrior Oisin the Otherworld, the mystical enchanted land of many Celtic myths.

In Irish myth, the Otherworld was created as the domain of the divine race of the Tuatha De Danann following their defeat by the Milesians (see page 55). The Milesians, it was decided, would rule the visible parts of Ireland, while the Dananns took possession of the invisible regions below ground and beyond the seas. This Otherworld was accessible through caves, lakes and above all the *sidhe* or fairy-mounds, the countless prehistoric burial mounds of Ireland such as those of the Boyne in

The handle of this 1st-century AD bronze cup from County Leitrim is a stylized representation of the head of a bird, probably a swan. Swans are often linked with the Otherworld in Irish myth.

County Meath. The Dagda, the tribal patriarch of the Dananns, divided the *sidhe* among his people. According to one story, the Dagda gave each of his offspring a *sidh* except for Oenghus, his son by the goddess Boann. The Dagda had Oenghus raised by Oenghus's half-brother Midir at the *sidh* of Bri Leith. Later, Oenghus went with Midir to demand a *sidh* from their father. The Dagda said that he had given out all the fairy-mounds, but told Oenghus to go to Newgrange, the *sidh* of Nuadu, a Danann king, and ask to stay a night and a day there. Nuadu agreed, but at the end of his stay Oenghus refused to move and lived at Newgrange thereafter.

For most of the time, life in the Otherworld consisted of hunting and feasting, and those who lived there knew neither pain nor sickness. Nor did they ever grow old, for which reason the Otherworld was also known as *Tir na n-Og*, the "Land of Youth". Each *sidh* possessed a magic cauldron that dispensed an inexhaustible supply of food, and also boasted some special wonder. There might be magic apple trees continually laden with fruit that granted immortality; or food and drink that restored the dead to life; or pigs that could be slaughtered and cooked in a cauldron one day and come back to life the next, to be eaten again; or magic potions that bestowed great wisdom.

Manannan, the god of the sea, was said to have built invisible barriers to keep mortals out of the Otherworld. Nevertheless, there are many stories of heroes and other individuals crossing into the Otherworld by accident, or being led there by

# The Mystic Hound

*"Of all the hounds he had seen in the world, he had seen no dogs the same colour as these. Their colour was a brilliant shining white, and their ears red."* King Pwyll of Dyfed was right to wonder at these strange dogs, for their master was Arawn, the ruler of Annwn, the magical Otherworld of Welsh mythology.

Dogs are among the animals most often connected with the Otherworld in Celtic myth. They may be harbingers of death, as the red-eared hounds of Annwn are sometimes said to be – red was associated with death, as seen vividly in the story of Da Derga's hostel (see page 31). In this tale, Da Derga is said to possess a pack of nine white hounds: white is another colour that indicates the supernatural in Celtic myth. Dog skeletons have been found at many sites, which suggests that they were involved in ritual sacrifice, possibly associated with the afterlife and the Otherworld. For the Celts, dogs were also believed to have magical healing qualities. It has been suggested that this is because they heal their own wounds by licking, but for whatever reason depictions of the animals are commonly found at Celtic healing sanctuaries. At one sanctuary, at Lydney in Gloucestershire, no fewer than nine canine images have been

A bronze hound from the Roman-period healing sanctuary to the god Nodens at Lydney, Gloucestershire.

discovered as offerings to the British god Nodens. Visitors to the sacred healing springs at the source of the river Seine in France (see page 33) would sometimes offer up to the goddess Sequana images of a person carrying a dog. Dogs are often the companions of mother goddesses.

magic animals or fairy women. In the tale of Mael Duin, the hero's ship contains more than the magic number of eighteen men and in consequence drifts into the Otherworld kingdom of Manannan, which did not lie below ground but was a group of enchanted islands.

The Tuatha De Danann, however, could move freely between the mortal world and their own domain. The Morrigan was one Danann who regularly left her *sidh* to oversee the fate of warriors, most notably Cuchulainn. At the festival of Samhain (October 31–November 1), the boundaries of the Otherworld came down altogether, and its inhabitants left their *sidhe* to roam freely among mortals, often causing havoc with their magic. For most

ordinary folk, Samhain was a time to stay at home and bolt the doors and windows, but it was not always possible to avert trouble. The hero Finn first came to the attention of the High King of Ireland by vanquishing an Otherworldly mischief-maker who regularly burnt down the royal seat at Tara. In later times, the gods and goddesses of the Otherworld became the fairy people of folk belief, just as the old Celtic feast of Samhain has survived down to the present day as Hallowe'en.

The land of Annwn, the magic underworld of Welsh mythology, is similar to the Irish Otherworld. It is a land of hunting, feasting, health and youth, ruled by King Arawn, who sometimes emerged into the mortal world on hunting expeditions with his

# Oisin and Niamh

*The visit of the warrior Oisin to the Otherworld is part of a tradition of stories in which heroes fall in love with fairy women. Niamh, an Otherworld princess, rode out of the mists on the shores of Lough Leane, where Finn and his warriors were hunting. "I have come for Oisin son of Finn," she declared. Oisin fell in love with Niamh at once and leapt onto the horse behind her. They rode off into the lough and entered the Otherworld.*

*Below*: Lough Leane, one of the Lakes of Killarney in present-day County Kerry and the scene of Oisin's departure for the Otherworld with the fairy woman Niamh.

Oisin and Niamh married, had three children and enjoyed every imaginable pleasure. Oisin lived for three centuries in the Otherworld without growing a day older. But he missed Ireland and his father. Even though Niamh had told him that things would not be the same as they had been when he left, Oisin still wanted to go back, so she warned him that while he was there he must not set foot on Irish soil. With a promise to return swiftly, Oisin rode back into the mortal world.

Niamh had been right. Finn's castle was nothing but an overgrown ruin, and Finn himself lived only in folktales. Oisin's heavy heart made him careless and, forgetting Niamh's warning, he got off his horse to wash at a trough. The moment his foot touched the ground, he aged three hundred years and fainted, a wizened old man. He came to in the arms of St Patrick, who had just arrived in Ireland. The saint tended the aged Oisin, who in his last years became a famous bard, telling stories of Finn that drew audiences from all over Ireland.

magical hounds. In the First Branch of the *Mabinogion,* King Pwyll of Dyfed exchanges places with Arawn for a year, and spends his time in Annwn "in hunting and song and carousal, and affection and discourse with his companions". After this there is a firm friendship between Annwn and the kingdom of Dyfed. According to the Second Branch of the *Mabinogion,* the first pigs to be seen in Britain came from Annwn and were given by Arawn to Pwyll's successor, Pryderi.

One of the treasures of Annwn was a magic cauldron of plenty. In one story, *The Spoils of Annwn,* Arthur and three boatloads of his men entered the underworld in an attempt to steal the cauldron. The raid was a complete disaster, however, and Arthur escaped from Annwn with only half a dozen of his companions. Arthur's experience points to the darker side of the Otherworld. When mortals ventured into it deliberately, they tended to encounter demons, monsters and other perils, rather than the land of bliss that greeted those who strayed into it or were invited or conducted there by one of its true inhabitants.

## Life after Death

The discovery in Celtic graves of such things as food, cauldrons and other domestic artefacts, as well as objects symbolizing the sun, suggests that the ancient Celts probably believed in some form of life after death. In Irish myth, the Otherworld was also the land of the dead, who were ruled by a god called Donn, the "Dark One". He was said to be the eldest son of Mil, the leader of the Milesians, who fell foul of the goddess Eriu by not wanting to name Ireland after her. Donn was drowned in the sea off southwestern Ireland, but after his death he became ruler of the dead and went to live in a *sidh,* a small island that is still called Tech nDuinn ("House of Donn"). From here, it was said, the dead would begin their journey to the Otherworld.

Donn may be identical with the figure of Da Derga ("Red God"), who features in a myth called *The Destruction of Da Derga's Hostel.* The "hostel" in question is one of a number of Otherworldly houses that appear in the Irish myths. According to the story, the High King of Ireland, Conaire, was predestined to die in this house. He journeyed inexorably towards it, despite various omens such as three riders in red on red horses. The climax of the story is a great battle in the hostel, during which Conaire is beheaded.

Conaire's champion, Mac Cecht, gave the severed head a drink of water, and it recited a brief poem before dying. There are echoes here of the Welsh story of Bran the Blessed, who was killed in a great battle and ordered his followers to cut his head off and take it to London. On the way, they sojourned for eighty years at Gwales, an Otherworldly island (perhaps Grassholm) off the Pembroke coast of Dyfed. Gwales recalls Donn's offshore *sidh* of Tech nDuinn. Here, as Bran had predicted, the head remained uncorrupted and talked as merrily as ever it did while he was still alive. The hero Cuchulainn was also said to have entered the Otherworld, and severed heads were among the things he saw there.

Magic pigs are not the only animals specifically associated with the Otherworld, as well as being simply the attributes of individual gods or goddesses. Others include dogs (see page 29) and swans. There are several myths in which magical Otherworld swans appear: in many cases they are metamorphosed humans, as in the stories of Midir and Etain (see page 69) and Oenghus and Caer (see page 70). Another story relates how the sea god Lir, the father of Manannan, went into self-imposed exile in a *sidh* in Ulster after failing to be chosen as king of the Otherworld. The successful candidate, Bobd Dearg, magnanimously presented Lir with his sister Aobh in recompense. Lir and Aobh were married and had two sets of twins (or three children in some variants). When Aobh died, Lir married her sister Aiofe, who was jealous of her stepchildren and turned them into swans. They were destined to remain swans for nine hundred years, until the coming of St Patrick, who freed them from the spell. When the saint restored them to human form they were old and wizened, but lived just long enough to be baptized into the new Christian religion.

# Gods and the Natural World

For the Celts, religion was inseparable from the world about them, and just about every feature of the landscape was imbued with some sacred significance. Bogs were evil. Fires caused by lightning were sacred. There was not a mountain, tree, river or spring that did not have its own spirit. The unknown lurked at every step. Amid these numinous surroundings it was unwise to tread carelessly, for fear of offending the gods. Even the conquering Roman legionaries were careful to make offerings to the unfamiliar deities of rivers, groves and forests that they encountered as they advanced through Gaul and Britain.

The wooded landscape around the Aber Falls (Rhaeadr Fawr) in Gwynedd would once have been typical of all Wales, where some of the Britons' most hallowed groves were to be found. At the time of the Roman conquest of Britain, the principal sanctuary of the British druids was a sacred grove on Anglesey.

The Celtic deities of the natural world were often synonymous with the places themselves: thus the name of the Gaulish god Vosegus was also the name of the mountains he personified, the Vosges in France. Rivers, the deities of which were almost always female, were particularly venerated as an essential source of life for farmers, upon whom in turn the wellbeing of the community depended. One of the most striking rivers in this respect is the Marne in eastern France, which is derived from Matrona ("Matron"), the title given to several great mother goddesses (see page 25). The cult of Souconna, the Gaulish goddess of the Saône at Lyon, was adopted by the Romans in Gaul, and her festival formed part of the great Gallo-Roman celebrations in honour of the god Lugus and the emperor Augustus on August 1. Among the other important Gaulish river goddesses was Sequana, goddess of the river Seine. In contrast, relatively few eponymous river goddesses are known from Britain and Ireland. Sabrina was the goddess of the Severn, Verbeia of the Wharfe in northeastern England and Boann of the Boyne.

Swords, shields and helmets were frequently cast into rivers and other bodies of water as offerings to deities: the famous episode where Bedivere throws King Arthur's sword Excalibur into a lake recalls this old Celtic practice. The Thames in London and the river Witham in Lincolnshire, for example, have yielded some of the finest Celtic weaponry yet discovered (see pages 16, 46 and 53). Both river names are of Celtic origin – Thames means "Dark" and Witham possibly "Forest River" – but whether these were also the names of their resident deities is not known. Many of the artefacts deposited in them appear to be too decorative to have been of practical use and may have been made especially as ritual offerings.

Among the commonest objects found in rivers and other bodies of water are swords which have been deliberately bent. The reason for this practice is not clear, but it may simply have been to render them useless to mortals tempted to steal them.

### Sacred Springs and Wells

The most sacred part of any river was the source, usually a spring, where the waters were seen to emerge mysteriously from the ground. Irish myth recounts how the river Boyne sprang from a sacred spring belonging to Nechtan, a water god. A magic hazel tree that overhung the well dropped its nuts into the water, imbuing it with great knowledge and wisdom (the nuts themselves were eaten by the Salmon of Knowledge). Only four people were permitted to visit the well: Nechtan himself and his three cupbearers. However, Nechtan's wife Boann breached the taboo and approached the well. Outraged by this trespass, its waters at once burst forth in a great gush which overwhelmed Boann and created a new river. The river took her name – the Boyne – and she became its goddess.

Springs were credited with great healing powers, and Gaul and Britain abounded with healing springs dedicated to some god or goddess. In his capacity as a god of healing, the Roman Apollo was identified with various Celtic gods, such as Belenus and Vindonnus, who were imbued with the same characteristics, and various springs were focal points for their cults. One of the most important shrines in Gaul was at the Sequana Spring, at the source of the Seine in Burgundy. Another spring, at Glanum in Provence, was sacred to the Celts, the Greeks and the Romans in turn. The local healing deity, Glanis, was worshipped there alongside three mother goddesses known as the Glanicae.

The chief sacred spring in Britain was Aquae Sulis ("Waters of Sulis", modern Bath), where the

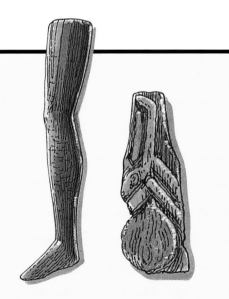

## The Sequana Spring

**The springs at the source of the river Seine in the Châtillon Valley, Burgundy, were the centre of a healing cult in honour of Sequana, the goddess of the river. In 1963 two hundred wooden votive offerings were recovered from the waters of the spring.**

The springs had been a Gaulish pilgrimage site for a long time before the Romans built a great temple complex at the place they called *Fontes Sequanae* ("The Springs of Sequana"). Pilgrims came from many miles around to make offerings to the goddess in return for a cure for their ills. They would ritually cleanse themselves in a pond before entering the main temple, in which stood a great bronze statue of Sequana.

Along with the usual type of offerings, such as coins and jewellery, the devotees would cast into the waters wooden models of the afflicted parts of the body for which they sought a cure.

**Drawings of a miniature leg and human internal organs, two of the many models of parts of the body carved in wood and deposited in the Sequana springs by pilgrims in hope of a cure.**

33

hot springs that attracted thousands of pilgrims in ancient times still bubble up from the ground to this day. The Romans built a great temple complex to Sulis, the native British goddess of the springs, whom they identified with their own goddess Minerva. A triad of Celtic goddesses called the Suleviae were among the other deities venerated at the shrine. The offerings thrown into the springs included many so-called "curse tablets", small folded tablets of lead upon which were scratched requests to the goddess to punish some offence committed against the worshipper. Some of these curses may seem entertainingly trivial to modern sensibilities – one devotee begs Sulis to avenge the theft of a cloak – but they give some insight into the extent to which Celtic deities were thought to be able to intervene in everyday life.

Further north, near Hadrian's Wall, British and Roman pilgrims deposited jewellery, miniature statues and thousands of coins in the sacred spring at Brocolitia, present-day Carrawburgh. Coventina, the goddess of this spring, was usually portrayed in the form of a Classical water nymph, and she sometimes appeared as a triple goddess. Evidence of the worship of Coventina has been found outside Britain as far away as the south of France.

The ancient veneration for springs and wells has survived in folklore, as seen in the widespread custom of casting coins into wishing wells. In some parts of Derbyshire, it is a traditional custom to "dress" (decorate) wells elaborately on certain holy days, while in Ireland and Scotland some people still tie rags to the branches of overhanging trees and bushes in order, they believe, to activate the curing powers of nearby wells and pools. Many of the springs and holy wells that are assigned to saints were doubtless associated with pagan gods, goddesses and spirits in pre-Christian times.

A Roman-period monument discovered at the spring of Carrawburgh, Northumberland. It bears the Latin dedication "To the Goddess Coventina" (*Deae Covventinae*).

## Sacred Trees and Groves

Trees were revered as symbols of seasonal death and regrowth, and they also formed a bridge between the earth and the heavens. The most sacred tree was the oak. The huge pillars that formed part of the many Romano-Celtic monuments to Jupiter were sometimes sculpted as stylized oaks. The druids would only collect their sacred mistletoe from oak trees, according to the Roman writer Pliny the Elder (AD23–79). He describes the ceremony involved in gathering the plant: "They prepare a sacrifice and a holy feast under the tree ... a priest dressed in white climbs the tree, cuts the mistletoe with a golden sickle and catches it in a white cloak."

Pliny goes so far as to derive the word "druid" itself from the Greek *drys*, "oak", and it may well derive from a related Celtic word. Oak groves were among the holiest of all druidic sacred places, and the word *nemeton* ("grove" or "sanctuary") is found in numerous ancient Celtic place-names, such as Nemetobriga ("Exalted Grove") in Spain, Drunemeton ("Oak Grove") in Galatia in Asia Minor, and in present-day Nymet and Nympton in Devon.

The sacred groves of Anglesey, the scene of human sacrifice according to Roman sources, may also have been oakwoods, since oak forests covered most of Wales in Roman times. Oak trees feature particularly in Welsh myth, where they are often associated with magic. In the story of Lleu, oak blossom is one of the flowers used to conjure up the flower-woman Blodeuwedd. Later, when Lleu is wounded by his enemy Gronw, he changes into an eagle that perches at the top of an oak tree. The tree is described as "a sanctuary for a fair lord" and appears to have magic properties, in that "neither rain nor heat affect it".

In Irish myths, the hazel enjoys much greater prominence than the oak as a supernatural tree.

# The Washer at the Ford

*At times rivers and streams possessed a sinister symbolism as the boundaries between life and death. One common theme is that of the Washer at the Ford – the war goddess who waited at a ford, sometimes in the form of a woman, sometimes as a crow or raven, and determined which of the warriors who passed would perish on the battlefield that day.*

A stylized bird, probably a crow or raven, drawn from a Spanish Celtic pot of *c.*100BC.

On their way to battle, a band of warriors stopped at a ford, where they beheld a terrible sight. A tall phantom woman, her eyes red and angry, glowered at them through grey, matted hair. At her feet, which were awash with blood, lay the mangled corpses of warriors, some so hideously disfigured that not even their mothers would have recognized them.

As the warrior band gaped in horror, the woman let out a hideous, shrieking laugh that sent a shiver of terror down their spines. Slowly, she raised her arm and pointed a bony finger at each man in turn. At last the chief of the band found the strength to approach the woman. With much effort, he forced himself to speak. "Who are you?" he asked.

"I?" she screeched, "I am the Morrigan, the Phantom Queen. Some call me the Washer at the Ford. I sleep on Mount Knocknarea, deep in the Cairn of Maeve. My work is to haunt all the streams of Ireland, washing away all the sins of men."

"Who, then," asked the war-chief, "are the sinful men who lie in this gory heap before us? Are they those you have killed and maimed today?"

The Morrigan cackled again. "I did not kill these men, nor have I so much as harmed a hair on their heads!" She peered deep into the warrior's eyes. "Look again at these dead warriors. They are the very men that stand behind you, as they will be this evening, after the battle. I am merely washing the blood from their limbs."

The chieftain looked again at the corpses, and began to make out the features of some of his comrades. The Morrigan slowly bent down to rummage among her gory bounty, then held up an object for the chief to see. He turned to look and beheld, dangling by bloody locks, his own severed head.

Hazels were especially linked with divine insight and knowledge, as in the stories of Boann and the Salmon of Knowledge. Apple trees feature in both the Welsh and Irish stories as trees of the Otherworld that bear fruit with magical properties. The tale of Mael Duin's voyage into the Otherworld recounts how three magic apples sustained his crew of eighteen for one hundred and twenty days. In the *Adventure of Conla,* a woman of the Otherworld gives the hero Conla an apple which always remains whole even though he eats from it for a month. In the Welsh tale of Culhwch, the hero's supernatural nature is hinted at by, among other things, the precious "apples of red gold" embroidered on his mantle. Avalon, the name of the mystic Otherworld which receives the dying King Arthur in the Arthurian legends, is derived from the Celtic word for "apple" (*afal* in Welsh). In his account of Arthur's life, Geoffrey of Monmouth actually calls Avalon "the Isle of Apples".

# The Great Festivals

The Celtic calendar appears to have been dominated by four great festivals which, in modified forms that play down their pagan origins, have survived in Irish culture down to the present day: Imbolg, Beltane, Lughnasad and Samhain.

The festivals mark the beginning of the seasons and relate to the fertility of the earth and of livestock. Their rituals aimed to ensure the growth and continuity of life. The sun was frequently the focus of the rituals, with bonfires being lit to emulate the sunlight in spring and to encourage warmth in autumn.

The Celtic year began on November 1 with the festival of Samhain, which means "Summer". It actually marked the end of summer, a time when farmers brought their animals down from the pastures and prepared for the winter ahead. The festival ran from the beginning of October 31 to the end of November 1, referred to in Irish texts as the "Three Nights of Samhain" – the Celts reckoned in nights rather than days. The middle night of October 31 (New Year's Eve) was a time of flux and transition when the boundaries between the natural world and the supernatural Otherworld became fluid and humans were best advised to stay indoors to avoid mischievous gods and spirits.

Part of a Gaulish calendar of *c.*10BC found at Coligny in France. It includes the month of *Samon* ("Summer", mid-October to Mid-November), marking summer's end and the Celtic New Year. The words *Trinux Samoni* refer to a festival no doubt corresponding to the Irish "Three Nights of Samhain" (October 31–November 1).

# Brigit

**The patron deity of the feast of Imbolg was the goddess Brigit. One of the most popular of all Irish deities, she may be a sovereignty goddess in origin: her name comes from the Celtic brig ("exalted").**

Brigit was the goddess of the province of Leinster, but she was worshipped in every part of Ireland. She was sometimes said to have two sisters of the same name, which links her with the Celtic triple mother goddesses (see page 25). Brigit was associated with fertility and the spring, and women in childbirth prayed to her. She oversaw the lactation of ewes and cattle and was a great healer. A patron of crafts and

**Brigit may be identical in origin to the British goddess Brigantia, seen here in a Romano-British carving. Brigantia, patron of the Brigantes tribe, gave her name to the river Brent in Middlesex.**

poetry, the goddess was also versed in the mystic arts of prophecy and divination.

With the arrival of Christianity, Brigit underwent a remarkable transition from a goddess to the premier woman saint of Ireland, with the same feast day, February 1. *The Life of Brigit,* her Latin biography, was written c.AD650. St Brigit, it said, was born in the household of a druid and performed miracles such as hanging her cloak on a sunbeam and multiplying provisions. She became a nun and founded the convent of Kildare, dying in AD524. The saint was said to possess cows that gave a lake of milk, and to feed the needy from an inexhaustible supply of food.

In Irish myth, the gods are especially active at Samhain. It was then that the Otherworldly Aillen regularly burned down the fort at Tara, and the god Oenghus met his beloved, Caer, at this time.

At Samhain the leaders of the provinces of Ireland would congregate at Tara, where, amid religious rituals and much feasting, diplomatic missions were carried out and political alliances cemented. All the fires of Ireland were extinguished and then relit to symbolize the end of the old year and the beginning of the new. In Christian times Samhain became All Hallows or All Saints' Day (November 1), preceded on October 31 by All Hallows' Eve, or Hallowe'en.

Imbolg, February 1, marked the start of spring and celebrated the birth of new livestock, particularly lambs. The name probably means "Sheep's Milk". Its patron goddess was Brigit, the daughter of the Dagda, and the festival became the feast day of her christianized successor, St Brigit (see above).

The great festival of light, Beltane ("Fire of Bel"), fell on May 1 and heralded the onset of summer. The presiding deity of the festival (probably identical with Belenus; see page 26) was welcomed by bonfires, singing and dancing, which celebrated the return of the sun's heat and renewed fertility. The festival persists as May Day.

The harvest festival of Lughnasad on August 1 was said to have been founded by the god Lugh in honour of his mother. The celebrations actually spanned the month from July 15 to August 15, and apart from religious rituals the highlights included all-Ireland games held annually at Tara. These survived well into Christian times: they were last held in 1169 under Rory O'Conor, the last High King of Ireland. Lughnasad is still celebrated in the guise of the Christian feast of Lammas, which consecrates the first fruits of the harvest. The Gaulish version of Lughnasad became the most important festival of Roman Gaul (see page 21).

# Knowledge and Wisdom

The gods and goddesses embodied everything in the Celtic universe, visible and invisible. The more knowledge of the universe that mortals acquired, therefore, the closer they came to understanding, and perhaps influencing, the gods. The cultivation of arcane knowledge and sacred wisdom was thus central to Celtic education. To qualify as a "man of learning", a would-be sage had to acquire vast amounts of lore that encompassed ritual, prophecy, divination, poetry, song, mythology and the entire body of religious and secular laws.

The *Book of Invasions* provides an insight into what sort of things a truly wise person would know. According to the book, the first person to acquire great knowledge was Fintan, the only person in Ireland to survive the biblical Flood. He hid in a cave above the river Shannon for five and a half thousand years, in which time he amassed monumental knowledge of the world. He learned the geography and history of the land, and the secrets of immortality, and knew of the coming of Christ in a future century. He also learned things that humans could never know, because he spent part of his life in the forms of an eagle, a falcon and a one-eyed salmon, Ruadh Rofessa, the "Omniscient Red One".

Many people went to Fintan to draw upon his knowledge. Once, during a boundary dispute, the High King of Ireland went to him to find out the original divisions of the country. Astonished to find himself the only historian in Ireland, Fintan summoned the island's seven wisest men and bestowed on them the knowledge of their own history. He explained to them that the country had been divided into five

**The design on this 1st-century AD Irish spoon recalls Ireland's division into four provinces and the centre, Meath. It may have been used for divination, perhaps to invoke a deity of the land.**

## Divination

*The Celts believed that with the correct knowledge and techniques, it was possible to divine the future. The most common form of augury involved animals.*

It was said that the druids could look at birds in flight and make prophecies based on the way they flew or the shape of their talons. The druids were able to look into the future by cracking open the bones of certain creatures, usually dogs, cats or "red" pigs, and chewing the marrow or bloody flesh.

In some rituals, a druid ate the flesh of a sacrificed animal, then slipped into a deep sleep, during which his totem ancestor or animal would appear to answer his questions about the future.

Druids were also said to gain prophetic knowledge from their own fingers. If they drummed the ends of their fingers while chanting, they could discover the past of any person or article that they touched. In myth, the hero Finn sucked his thumb to activate knowledge acquired by eating a magic salmon.

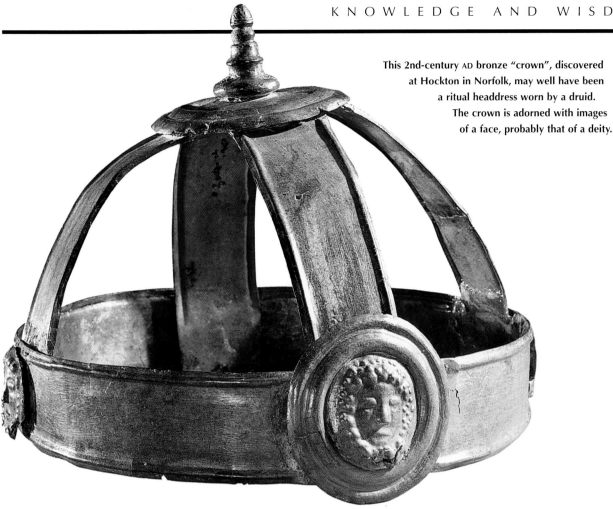

This 2nd-century AD bronze "crown", discovered at Hockton in Norfolk, may well have been a ritual headdress worn by a druid. The crown is adorned with images of a face, probably that of a deity.

provinces, each with its own character. Ulster was said to be the home of great warriors and Leinster of prosperity; the home of music and mystery was Munster, while knowledge and magic resided in Connacht. In the centre was Meath, the royal capital and seat of all wisdom.

In his salmon form, Fintan may be identical with the Salmon of Knowledge eaten by the young hero Finn. The salmon's flesh bestowed universal wisdom, and the bard Finnegas spent many years fishing for it. The element *fin* in all these names is connected with the acquisition or possession of knowledge, and it has been suggested that Fintan, Finnegas and Finn derive from the earlier Find, the divine spirit of wisdom, whose name means "Fair" or "Bright" and perhaps also "Enlightened". Little literature survives about Find, but we know that he was a triple god embodying the three ages of humankind: youth, maturity and old age. As a god of youth, he may be related to the god Maponus.

## Druids and Bards

The druids, the Celtic priestly caste, were a pervasive influence in Celtic society. As religious officials they interceded between this world and the gods, using arcane rituals in which sacrifice – sometimes of humans – played an important part, to predict auspicious dates for harvests, wars, coronations and a host of other events vital to the community's well-being. But druids were more than mere diviners. They also acted as judges, officiating in criminal trials, boundary disputes, divorces and inheritance wrangles. On top of this, they were the guardians of Celtic tradition, disseminating centuries of accumulated legend and ritual. The oak tree was central to many druidic rituals, and the word druid itself may come from a Celtic word for oak that is related to the Greek *drys* and the English *tree*.

Being a druid was a high-status position. "Large numbers of young men flock to them for instruction," wrote Caesar, "and they are held in great honour by the people." The druids travelled freely, and tribes who were at war with each other would always give peaceful passage to a druid. Druids were exempt from military service and did not have to pay war-taxes.

There is some dispute, however, between the Classical commentators and their later interpreters about whether there were druids throughout the Celtic lands, which stretched from the Iberian peninsula to Asia Minor. Writing two centuries apart, the Roman statesman Cicero (106–47BC) and the Greek geographer Ptolemy (c.AD140) both mention large conventions of druids at the sanctuary of Drunemeton in "Galatia", presumed to be the Celtic land in what is now Turkey. However, some experts think that druids probably did not get as far east as Asia Minor, and have pointed out that the two authors call the Celts *Galatai* or *Galatae,* which could also mean just the Gauls. The "Drunemeton" of Cicero and Ptolemy, therefore, might not be the one in Asia Minor but some great sanctuary in Gaul, probably in the territory of the Carnutes, along the middle reaches of the river Loire, where Caesar claimed that the Gaulish druids had their primary centre. Caesar reported that the druids originated in the British Isles, where Gaulish novice druids were often sent for training.

The skills of the druids fell into three categories: the receiving and holding of knowledge past, present and future; the regulation of daily life, including political, medical, scientific and legal learning; and the ability to communicate with the gods through ritual and sacrifice, in order to divine and influence future events. Novices, probably girls as well as boys, left home often as young as nine or ten and travelled to distant forest groves to begin their druidical education. The training period could last up to twenty years, there was so much information to commit to memory – and druids must have had astonishing memories, since they wrote none of their lore down but passed it on from generation to generation solely by word of mouth.

The druids were accomplished astronomers with a sophisticated knowledge of mathematics and natural science. Caesar himself conceded that they had "much knowledge of the stars and their motion, of the size of the world, and the movement of heaven and the stars". They devised a sophisticated lunar calendar with months of twenty-nine or thirty days, with each month divided into two half-months. The calendar was reckoned in nights rather than days, and had intercalary periods to keep it in line with the solar year.

More routinely, people often turned to the druids to settle legal arguments. If anyone ignored their judgments, they had the power to ban people from religious rituals. This was a heavy penalty, since excommunicated people were complete outcasts from society, shunned by others "for fear that they may get some harm from contact with them", as Caesar reported.

While exempt from fighting themselves, the druids taught warriors the rules of combat. They also instructed rulers in the duties and etiquette of kingship. They acted as mediators between warring tribes and their word often had more sway than that of a king or chief. The first-century AD Roman writer Pliny claimed that druids carried a magic egg made from the bodily secretions of vipers. The egg was said to ensure that the owner was always welcome among princes and true in his or her judgments.

The druids were divided into various groups, although it is difficult to be sure of their precise hierarchy and functions. Women druids, whom the Romans sometimes employed as diviners, may have formed a group of their own. In myth, female druids often play an important part in the education of heroes such as Cuchulainn, who received his military training at the hands of the druid Scathach on her Scottish island of Skye.

Other categories included priests who specialized in particular ceremonies, hermits, court druids, and bards. Bards were immensely important in Celtic society, although not all of them underwent the full druidic education. Even if they chose not to specialize, however, all druids were trained as bards and learnt to memorize and recite vast quantities of incantations, sacred lore and mythology in verse form. It was said that a bard's inspiration resided in the heart and blood, while insight was contained in a vein at the back of the head. The rigorous bardic training included being taught the art of interpreting riddles, a prestigious skill which displayed the bard's superior powers of perception.

Some bards inherited the gift of prophecy, while others developed it in the course of their training. In Irish myth, bards sometimes fall asleep on a fairy mound or hill and dream of a *leanon sidh* or "learning-fairy", a fairy muse who granted them the gift of divination and poetry.

Part of the bard's function was to prepare and update genealogies, chant traditional poems, and compose new ones to mark special occasions – births, weddings, deaths, battles, cattle-raids, the installations of kings. Honouring the bard's performance was believed to assure the listener's good fortune. Through their incantations, bards could also exorcise ghosts and evil spirits, control the movement of rats and drive out sickness. When a bard was displeased, however, his savage satires could cause red patches or blisters to break out on the subject's face. As late as 1414, the English viceroy in Ireland, Sir John Stanley, was alleged to have died as a result of poisoning caused by a bard's satirical invective.

With the coming of Christianity, it was the bards who passed on the old myths to Christian scribes. St Patrick himself was said to have blessed the mouth of the bard Dubhthach, who accompanied him on his mission. As storytellers, bards retained their importance in Celtic society well into the seventeenth century. The revival of the Welsh bardic tradition was a feature of the nineteenth century's renewed interest in the Celts.

**An 18th-century engraving of an imaginary druidic festival at Stonehenge, which was once thought, mistakenly, to have been a "temple" of the druids.**

# Ritual and Sacrifice

The twin functions of divination and assuring the future were the most popular of the druids' activities, and generally included some form of sacrifice. Much is often made of the Celts' propensity for sacrifice, which in Roman texts is distorted into wholesale massacres of human beings: Caesar claimed that the Gauls would build a huge wicker model of a man and fill it with victims before setting the structure alight. The druids did sometimes sacrifice humans, but far fewer than the Romans claimed. Most sacrifices involved the killing of animals or the ritual destruction of a weapon.

The first-century AD Roman writer Pliny noted that the Celts sacrificed bulls and oxen, and the practice is well attested. The installation at Tara of the High King of Ireland, for example, involved a ritual called the "Bull-Sleep", in which a white bull was slaughtered. A druid consumed some of the bull's blood and flesh before going to sleep wrapped in the animal's hide. The dreams he had during this ritual slumber were said to indicate whether or not the correct person had been chosen as king.

*Below*: The "skull gateway" to the Gaulish sanctuary of Roquepertuse in southern France. The skulls may be evidence of human sacrifice.

*Above*: The 3rd-century BC Gundestrupp cauldron. Cauldrons were used to catch the blood of sacrifice victims and for boiling flesh.

Inanimate objects were also offered to the gods. Deep pits, perhaps conceived of as entrances to the Otherworld, were filled with offerings of jewels, pottery and weapons which had been ceremonially broken before being thrown in. Weaponry was also often deposited in rivers and lakes.

Celtic funerals in particular were "magnificent and expensive", according to Caesar. Archaeological discoveries show that the Celts buried their nobles with chariots, jewellery, rich fabrics and vessels of various kinds. Some graves have yielded dogs, hares, birds and even whole teams of horses complete with cart. There is evidence that entire clans would gather for funeral banquets and ritual processions, at the end of which spears might be ceremonially hurled into the dead person's grave. Around 100BC there was a growing trend for

# Bog Burials

**The Celts regularly made ritual deposits in bogs and marshes, perhaps to appease the gods or spirits who were thought to suck in unwary visitors. Among the offerings were cauldrons, weapons, chariots – and human beings.**

Bodies of both men and women, mainly under forty years old, have been found in bogs. The most famous, from Denmark, is "Tollund Man", who had been ritually garotted and was found naked apart from a cap and girdle. He was probably a Celt, because the corpse of a similarly executed ancient Briton was recovered from Lindow Marsh near Manchester. He too was naked, except for a fox-fur armband. Both garottes had been knotted in the same way, and an examination of the two men's stomachs revealed pollen of mistletoe, a plant sacred to the druids, who probably prepared a last ritual meal for victims. The Lindow man had been knocked out by blows to the back of the head, then garotted to death, before having his throat cut and being flung face down into the bog.

**The body recovered from Lindow Marsh. The bog had preserved the body remarkably well, and his skin, nails and general health revealed that he was probably a high-status individual.**

cremation, so little evidence of funeral customs from after this time survives, except for the accounts of such foreign observers as Caesar. "They put on the fire everything they reckon to have been precious to the departed," he reported, "even living creatures." He adds that only a generation before he was writing, dependants and slaves might also have been thrown into the flames.

Such ceremonies may have been intended as an appropriately grand send-off to the Otherworld, where the dead would arrive equipped with the familiar objects and creatures that had been useful to them in the mortal world. Unfortunately, the unwritten lore attached to these splendid funerary rituals passed, with druidism, into oblivion. We are left to guess why, for example, the skulls of beheaded corpses were stored at the southern French sanctuary of Roquepertuse; or why, at other shrines, bodies were dismembered, decapitated, flayed and stripped of flesh before being piled up.

Military victories had their own ritual etiquette. The winners of a battle would sacrifice any living creatures they had captured, and the Romans were surprised to find that, unlike many armies, the Celts did not keep the plunder of battle for themselves but dedicated it all to the gods. Any warrior who tried to keep his booty was punished with torture.

In peacetime, too, the Celts believed that it was impious to touch any valuables intended as a gift to the gods. Writing in the first century BC, Diodorus Siculus commented that in the temples of Gaul "a great amount of gold is openly on show as an offering to the gods, and no one dares to touch it through religious fear."

The Celts attributed supernatural and mystical qualities to a variety of domestic and wild animals. The burial of animals with their owners perhaps demonstrates that they too were expected to have an existence after death. Animals are associated with healing and are often found at curative springs. Cliodna, an Otherworld queen, possessed three birds whose song restored health. In Celtic myth, various beasts are linked with the Otherworld and possess special wisdom which they use to help mortals. Animals are also helpers and bringers of good fortune. Fantastic creatures sometimes represent opposition or tests set by supernatural agents. There are many tales of people transforming from human to animal shape.

*Below*: Ram-horned snakes and dragon-like griffins adorn the Gundestrupp cauldron (see page 42). Horns and snakeskins renew themselves, making the ram-horned snake a potent fertility symbol. Dragons were slain by such heroes as Finn and Tristan.

*Left*: Probably owing to their colour and carrion habits, crows and ravens were linked with darkness and death – especially death in battle. War-goddesses often took the shape of these birds. This brooch of *c.*450BC was found in a tomb in Austria.

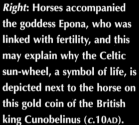

*Right*: Horses accompanied the goddess Epona, who was linked with fertility, and this may explain why the Celtic sun-wheel, a symbol of life, is depicted next to the horse on this gold coin of the British king Cunobelinus (*c.*10AD).

*Left:* For the Celts, bulls were important symbols of strength, wealth and virility: this late 1st-century BC bronze bull was buried in the grave of a British chieftain. In the Irish epic *The Cattle Raid of Cooley,* a white bull and a brown bull symbolize respectively the sovereignty of the opposing kingdoms of Ulster and Connacht (see pages 56–62).

*Above:* The White Horse cut into the chalk downs near Uffington in Oxfordshire is of uncertain date, but resembles Bronze Age Celtic images. It may mark some real event or represent a horse deity. In Celtic myth, white often has supernatural overtones.

# BATTLES OF THE HEROES

The year was AD82. Agricola, the Roman governor of Britain, stood on the Mull of Kintyre in southwestern Scotland and contemplated the land that lay just eighteen kilometres across the sea. The Gauls and Britons had put up fierce resistance, but in the end the might of Rome had proved invincible. One legion and a few auxiliaries, he thought, would bring Ireland under imperial rule. For some reason, however, Agricola chose not to invade. This decision ensured for many centuries the isolation of Europe's last unconquered Celtic enclave.

The Celts of Ireland, or Gaels, had arrived in two swathes, one from the Continent, the other probably from northern Britain. When they came remains unknown, but by the early centuries AD the Gaels had become the island's dominant people. They also established kingdoms in what later became known as Scotland and Wales. The Britons called the raiders by a word of uncertain meaning that the Irish, who spoke a different variety of Celtic from the Britons, adopted as *Goidel.* In time it became *Gaidheal*, from which comes the English "Gael".

When Ireland's pagan traditions finally succumbed to outside influences they did so not to the force of arms but to the gentler persuasion of Christian monks. The agent of change was Patrick (AD385–462), the son of a Roman official in Britain. Patrick established Christianity in Ireland and in the following centuries it steadily ousted or assimilated the old beliefs. But Ireland's monks were diligent chroniclers of their own history. By the twelfth century they had turned out a body of writing now grouped for modern convenience into four major anthologies: the Mythological Cycle, the Ulster Cycle, the Finn or Fenian Cycle and the Kings Cycle. This "history" was a brew of ancient myth and legend – tales of gods, demons, heroes, lovers, magic animals and sacred places – plus the occasional historical fact. The Ulster Cycle in particular has been called "a window on the Iron Age". Its accounts of feasting, chariot fights and rich costumes reflect a Celtic society recognizably similar to that which Caesar had encountered in Gaul more than a thousand years earlier.

*Left*: This 4th-century BC bronze belt decoration from Slovenia shows an armed Celtic warrior. His oval shield with its large boss is like many found all over the Celtic world.

*Opposite, above*: A British horned bronze helmet of c.50BC. It was dredged from the river Thames in London, where it may have been deposited as an offering to a war deity.

*Opposite, below*: An elaborately decorated bronze disc from the Marne region of eastern France. It once adorned the chariot or harness of a Gaulish warrior who lived c.400BC.

47

# The Great Invasions

The *Mythological Cycle* tells of the foundation and early settlement of Ireland, mostly through the *Leabhar Gabhala* ("Book of Invasions"), one of a number of works that make up the cycle. As a story of beginnings, it is by no means comprehensive. The Gaels seem not to have been concerned with cosmic origins. Their tales contain no stories of how the world and humankind were created, no conquests of Chaos and no Gardens of Eden. Perhaps the druids had answers to these questions, but if so, no trace of them has survived.

The *Book of Invasions* was compiled by monks in the twelfth century. It chronicles the successive races who were said to have invaded and colonized Ireland, ending with the invasion of the Milesians – the ancestors of the Gaels – who claimed the land for all time. The book details the legacy of each people: for example, agriculture and the arts of brewing, music and metal-working. It describes not only how Ireland was peopled and civilized, but also its physical creation. From being an almost fea-tureless landmass, Ireland emerged as a country of rivers, lakes, mountains, islands and plains, all of which were imbued with mythological significance.

The monks who assembled the *Book of Invasions* discarded any pagan myths of cosmic beginnings that they may have come across. Instead, they set the saga against a background drawn from the Bible which begins at the time of the great flood recounted in Genesis. The leader of the first invasion, Bith, is said to be a son of Noah. Bith (who is not mentioned in the Bible) was refused a place in his father's ark and was downcast until his daughter, Cessair, advised him to build an idol. This he did, whereupon the idol gave him the same advice that God had given Noah: there would be a great flood, and Bith must build a boat if he was to avoid destruction. It was sound counsel except for one detail: the idol was not able to say when the flood would come. Bith had nothing to lose. He constructed the boat and sailed away with two men, Ladra and Fintan, and fifty-one female passengers, including Cessair.

They sailed for seven years until they reached Ireland. The three men divided the land and the women among them, and Fintan took Cessair as his wife. Bith and Ladra soon died – the latter of an "excess of women" – and shortly afterwards the flood arrived and wiped out the entire population. Only Fintan survived, and he lived for another five and a half thousand years by changing himself, successively, into a salmon, an eagle and a hawk. Through centuries and generations Fintan gained an unrivalled overview of Ireland, advising its inhabitants about the history and names of places.

Ireland

Giant's Causeway
Tory Island
ULSTER
Lough Neagh
Emhain Macha (Navan Fort)● ●Armagh
▲ BEN BULBEN
SLIGO
MEATH
CUAILNGE (COOLEY)
CONNACHT
Magh Tuiredh (Moytirra) ●
Kells ● ●Newgrange
Boyne ●Tara
Lough Corrib
Shannon ●Durrow
Aran Islands
Inishmore
▲ SLIEVE BLOOM
LEINSTER
KERRY
Lough Leane
MUNSTER
▲ **Hill or range of hills**

# The Sources of Irish Myth

*The Irish sagas are the oldest works of Celtic literature, yet their existence is something of an irony. For it was only when Christianity replaced druidism that writing became widely accepted. Thus, some of the best sources for Celtic paganism came into being as a direct result of its demise.*

Irish myths were probably being recorded in the eighth century or earlier, possibly written on bark in ogham, a Gaelic script consisting of slashes and dashes. The only extant examples of ogham, however, are on stone monuments, and the bulk of the mythological record consists of the four cycles drawn up by twelfth-century Christian scribes (see page 47). The organization of these texts as cycles is convenient but artificial. If the original myths were grouped at all it was probably by theme – births, deaths, raids, conceptions and wooings. Some tales may have been fluid creations, differing from one telling to the next. The monastic scribes reworked the spoken word into a literary genre that was designed to be read aloud to royal and noble audiences. Inconsistencies abounded as writers worked to condense a host of versions into a single whole. Over the years, as more copies were made and the original Old Irish became old-fashioned, more errors crept in. This gives some idea of the problems

facing modern interpreters. Alongside this scribal activity there was also an unbroken oral tradition. Its importance to the understanding of Irish myth was realized in the nineteenth and twentieth centuries, when the decline of the Irish language began to alarm folklorists. As a result, many more old tales were recorded which might have been lost for all time.

The monks who recorded Irish myth assimilated some pagan elements into Celtic Christianity. The most famous example of this is the goddess Brigit, who became Ireland's premier woman saint, St Brigit (also called Bridget or Bride; see page 37). In this modern portrait she appears with the historical figures of St Patrick and St Columba.

He had to wait three centuries, however, before he had anyone to advise. It was then that the second invasion took place, led by his distant kinsman Partholon. Descended from Noah's son Japheth (the traditional ancestor of the Europeans), Partholon lived in Greece. He had killed his mother and his father in the hope of inheriting their kingdom, but when his ambitions were dashed he had set sail with twenty-four couples and landed in the southwest corner of Ireland. The Ireland he found was empty and uncultivated and had just three lakes, nine rivers and one plain. Partholon's crew soon set about bringing civilization to the island. They cleared the land, introduced livestock and the art of brewing, built houses and bred children.

Before long, four new plains were created through their endeavours and other features emerged with unnerving suddenness. When Partholon's son Rury was buried, for example, the earth burst open to form a new lake, which was named Lough Rury in his honour.

As well as giving the land physical shape, Partholon gave it a political dimension. During his reign it was divided into five provinces: Munster in the southwest, Connacht in the west, Leinster in the east, Ulster in the north and, at the heart of them all, Mide or Meath, which means "Centre". Meath was the seat of the historical High Kings of Ireland, whose capital, Tara, lay within its bounds. In spite of its name, Meath actually lay in east-central Ireland – the area covered approximately by present-day counties Meath and Westmeath. It ceased to exist as a province after the all too real invasions of the English in the twelfth century.

All was not well in Partholon's Ireland. He and his people faced problems from a race of monsters called the Fomorians. When and how the Fomorians arrived in Ireland is not recounted and they are not numbered among the colonizing races. Against them, Partholon struggled for control of Ireland. He and the Fomorians fought many battles, and eventually Partholon succeeded in containing the Fomorians on Tory Island off the coast of Donegal.

In spite of his success against the demons, Partholon's people were doomed. Their end came not in battle but in the form of a mysterious plague that steadily wiped them out one by one. This story of pestilence rings true – devastating plagues occur with almost monotonous regularity in the historical chronicles of the Irish kings.

As with the firstcomers to Ireland, though, there was one survivor: Partholon's nephew, Tuan. For twenty-two years he wandered through the land, scavenging food wherever he could. As he wandered he grew older and more decrepit. In due course, like Fintan before him, he transformed

A Gaulish statue of an eagle from a sanctuary at Roquepertuse, France, c.250BC. Celtic myth links the bird with metamorphosis: Fintan, Tuan and Lleu Llaw Gyffes (see page 90) all turned into eagles in the course of their adventures.

# The Fomorians

*Successive waves of Ireland's invaders battled the forces of violence and evil, as represented by the Fomorians. The inhuman wickedness of this monstrous race was represented by their misshapen physical appearance: they were variously described as possessing one leg, one arm, or one eye.*

Like Partholon, the Fomorians were said to be descendants of Noah. But their forefather was Ham, who had been cursed by Noah. As a result, his offspring developed into monsters – one account claimed that they each had three heads, three rows of teeth running from ear to ear, and bones without joints. A Fomorian could eat an ox and a pig at a sitting. Banished by Partholon to Tory Island, they continued to menace Ireland until their defeat at the second battle of Moytirra by the Tuatha De Danann.

Although generally malevolent, the Fomorians were also skilled farmers. The Tuatha De Danann were good artisans, but understood nothing about agriculture, and had to acquire this knowledge from the Fomorians in order to complete the process of civilizing Ireland.

**A Gaulish stone monster with two severed heads, from a sanctuary at Linsdorf in eastern France, *c.*200BC. It has been suggested that such sculptures symbolize the triumph of death, represented by the monsters, over mortals.**

himself – into a stag, a boar, an eagle, and finally into a salmon (the stories of Tuan and Fintan may simply be variants of the same tale). In this last guise he was caught and eaten many centuries later by a queen, then reborn as her son. The new-born Tuan was able to recite the whole history of Ireland from the coming of Partholon. Salmon and knowledge are closely linked in Irish myth (see page 63).

Among the first events Tuan recited was the coming of Nemed, his cousin and therefore another of Noah's descendants. Nemed arrived thirty years after Partholon and had an unpromising start. He had sailed for Ireland in a fleet of thirty-two ships, but after eighteen months lost at sea, only nine people stepped onto Ireland's shores: Nemed, four men and four women. Still, their numbers grew, until there were eight thousand and sixty of them.

Nemed defeated the Fomorians three times in battle, but after his death they returned once again to plague the land. In retaliation Nemed's people launched a fierce attack on Tory Island and killed the Fomorian king. Victory, however, was bought at a price: only thirty of Nemed's men survived. In despair, they took to the seas in search of a new homeland. Some headed for Britain, some for the "northern isles of the world", and some for Greece. Those of Nemed's people who set out for Greece found that the sanctuary they encountered was less than they had hoped for. On reaching Thrace they were enslaved. They were called Firbolgs, a name said to mean "Bag Men", from the bags in which they carried soil from Thrace's fertile valleys to the rocky mountains. Their descendants escaped by making the bags into coracles and sailing for home.

Of all the peoples said to have preceded the arrival of the Gaels, the Firbolgs are perhaps the most likely to have existed. There is evidence of a pre-Celtic population of Ireland and it has been suggested that the Firbolgs were derived from these people, who worshipped a god called Builg: their name would then mean "People of Builg". Another theory is that they may be related to a northern Gaulish tribe, the Belgae, some of whom are known to have migrated from Gaul to Britain in the late years BC. Whatever their origins there is a distinctly human quality to the Firbolgs. They have few of the epic characteristics of their predecessors or the magical ones of their immediate successors: the Tuatha De Danann.

**The Tuatha De Danann were famed as musicians. This figure of a harpist, possibly a god, is from Brittany (c.70BC).**

## The Tuatha De Danann

The Tuatha De Danann ("People of the Goddess Danu"), or "Dananns", were a divine race said to be descended from an earth goddess called Danu. They are especially interesting because many of them can be linked to Celtic gods known from Gaul and elsewhere. For obvious reasons, the Christian monks who rewrote the myths toned down their divine status and presented the Tuatha De Danann as a tribe whose chief figures had particular divine or magical attributes. Dian Cecht, for example, was their doctor, and his magic could restore the dead to life. Goibhniu, the smith, made weapons which always hit their target. He has a counterpart in the Welsh smith god Gofannon, who features in the story *Culhwch and Olwen* in the *Mabinogion*. The Morrigan was the goddess of war. Manannan was the god of the sea, who could raise fearful storms and tempests. Ogma, the poet, was said to have invented the Irish ogham alphabet and is clearly related to Ogmios, the Gaulish god of eloquence.

The king of the Tuatha De Danann was Nuadu, who had links with the British god Nodens and probably also the Welsh figure Nudd or Lludd (see page 98). In Roman times there was a great healing sanctuary dedicated to Nodens at Lydney in Gloucestershire, and it is interesting that Nuadu is associated with bodily perfection – he was initially chosen as king on the grounds that he was the most physically perfect of the Dananns. Presiding over the entire clan was the tribal patriarch, the Dagda or "Good God", whose huge club slew enemies at one end and brought them back to life with the other.

The skills of the Tuatha De Danann were magical, yet their personalities were very human. They quarrelled, made up, killed each other, repented, got drunk, slept with each other's wives, could be angry or calm, jealous or generous. In other respects, too, they reflected ordinary Celtic society: they were good musicians, they were accomplished craftsmen, and they bowed to the judgment – and sometimes the superior power – of their druids.

The Tuatha De Danann were said to be the descendants of those followers of Nemed who had fled to the northern islands of the world. They had

# The Battle of Moytirra

**Moytirra in Sligo witnessed two of the greatest battles in Irish myth. The first ended in the defeat of the Firbolgs and the establishment of the Tuatha De Danann as rulers of Ireland.**

When the Firbolgs refused a Danann demand to give up half of Ireland, conflict was inevitable. The battle did not take place for three months, because the Firbolgs needed this period to copy the fine javelins of the Dananns. Similarly, the Dananns spent the time copying the heavy spears of the Firbolgs. The battle finally began on midsummer's day. For three days the armies fought and many were slain, but neither side gained the upper hand. At the end of each day, doctors bathed the wounded in healing herbs that restored them in time for the next day's fighting. On the fourth day the Dananns began to push back the Firbolgs. At this crucial point, the Firbolg king became so thirsty that he left the field to find water. A Danann force set off in pursuit and after a fierce fight killed him. The Danann king, Nuadu, now offered peace and the Firbolgs accepted. For him, however, it was no victory. In battle he had lost an arm, and his people could accept only a physically perfect king. Nuadu was obliged to abdicate.

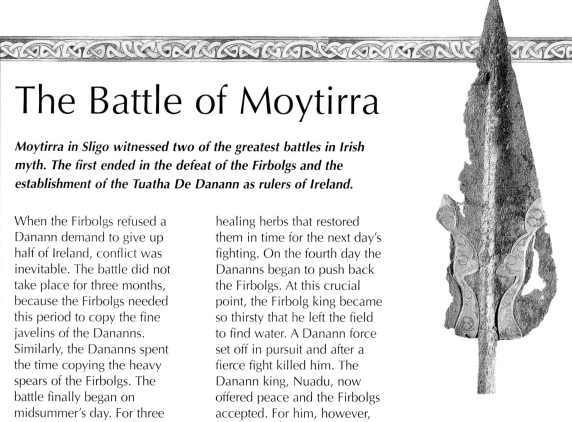

An iron spearhead with decorative bronze panels, produced *c.*200BC and deposited in the Thames in London, probably as a ritual offering.

settled in a mythical land of four cities – Falias, Gorias, Finias and Murias – each of which gave them a treasured talisman. From Falias was said to have come the historical *Lia Fail*, the "Stone of Destiny", on which the High King of Ireland was inaugurated at Tara. It was said that the stone gave a shout to confirm the legitimacy of the monarch. From Gorias came an invincible sword, from Finias a magic spear and from Murias an unempting cauldron which yielded an endless supply of food. Bearing this mixture of superhuman skills and human emotions, the People of Danu set off for Ireland in a magic cloud, which eventually landed in western Connacht.

Initially, relations were friendly between the newcomers and the Firbolgs, who sent an embassy to find out about the strangers. The Dananns did likewise, with both parties making a formal exchange of weapons. But then the Dananns demanded that the two peoples divide Ireland peacefully between them. The Firbolgs refused, and the two sides met in battle on the plain of Magh Tuiredh or Moytirra, in present-day County Sligo. Nuadu lost an arm in the battle, but the Firbolgs were defeated and their king, Eochaid mac Erc, was killed. The Dananns seized the Firbolg capital, Tara. Finally, according to one account, the Dananns allowed the defeated Firbolgs to retain Connacht, where they were left to live in peace while the Dananns occupied the rest of the island. In another account, the Firbolgs were driven from the mainland, but they continued to rule in the Aran Islands and built the fort of Dun Aonghusa on Inishmore.

The way was now clear for a climactic conflict between the Tuatha De Danann and the one race that still stood in their way: the Fomorians.

## The Tyranny of Bres

Dian Cecht made a new arm for Nuadu out of silver to replace the one he had lost at the Battle of Moytirra. But only a real arm would do and Nuadu was not reinstated. In his place was elected Bres, a man of great physical beauty. Unfortunately – unknown to the Dananns – he was also half-Fomorian, and his reign turned out to be a disaster. He was mean and inhospitable – faults considered unforgivable by the Irish – and allowed the Fomorians to terrorize the land. The Dananns were enslaved and even the Dagda was forced to dig trenches for Bres. In Irish myth, the prosperity of the land was linked to its ruler: if the king was physically or morally flawed, then the country would decline. So it was that under Bres, Ireland grew barren and desolate. Remedy came in the person of a poet, Coirbre, who lambasted Bres in a satirical poem. In ancient Ireland, satirical verse was believed to act like a magic spell. Coirbre's attack was literally a blistering satire – it made Bres come out in hideous boils. Robbed of his physical beauty, he was obliged to abdicate, to general relief.

Bres went to Tory Island to conspire with the giant Fomorian king, Balor of the Evil Eye. In the middle of his forehead Balor had one huge eye that destroyed everything it saw. To avert mass devastation Balor usually kept his eye shut, but in an emergency his men would prop it open – his eyelid was so heavy that he could not lift it himself.

Balor feared only one thing: a druid's prophecy that he would be killed by his own grandson. To prevent this, Balor kept his daughter and only child, Eithne, under lock and key on the island. However, with the aid of druid magic, a Danann lord named Cian made Balor's daughter pregnant with triplets. Balor gave orders for the babies to be drowned, but one, a boy, was washed up alive on Danann territory and raised by a smith. This boy was Lugh, the eventual saviour of the land.

Nuadu, in the meantime, had tired of his silver arm and approached Dian Cecht's son Miach, who was an even better physician than his father. Miach grew Nuadu a new arm (and was promptly killed by Dian Cecht out of jealousy). Nuadu was restored to the kingship, but he was unable to break the

The skill of Irish craftsmen was such that the idea of making Nuadu an arm out of metal might not have seemed unusual to Irish audiences. This bronze arm of uncertain date once housed the relics of an early Irish saint, a certain St Lactin.

power of the Fomorians. At this point Lugh presented himself before Nuadu at Tara.

Lugh possessed an astounding range of skills, like the great Celtic god Lugus to whom he is related (see page 19). Lugus was a god of light, and Lugh's face was said to be "like the setting sun, too bright to look on". As Nuadu said, "the like of him never came to Tara before." He was a great carpenter, smith, harpist, poet, magician, steward and warrior. Lugh rallied the Dananns and confronted the Fomorians at Moytirra, the scene of the defeat of the Firbolgs. The fighting was fierce and bloody, and Balor's eye wrought havoc among the Dananns, killing Nuadu and many others. A spear thrown by Balor's wife badly wounded the Dagda.

Amid the carnage, Lugh challenged Balor. "Open my eye!" cried the Fomorian. But as the lid was raised, Lugh hurled a slingshot at his grandfather with such force that the eye burst out of the back of Balor's head, turning its lethal gaze upon his own troops. The remaining Fomorians were driven into the sea, never to return. Lugh became king and prosperity returned to the land.

**Two warriors fighting, a design from a pot made *c.*100BC by Spanish Celts. These were the first Celtic people to appear in written accounts: Himilco, a Carthaginian who may also have visited Britain and Ireland, wrote about them *c.*425BC.**

## The Coming of the Gaels

The rule of the Tuatha De Danann lasted until the coming of Ireland's fifth, and last, race of invaders. These people were known as the "Sons of Mil" or Milesians, from their mythical leader Mil Espaine. His name is an Irish version of the Latin *Miles Hispaniae* ("Soldier of Spain") and apparently reflects an ancient Roman belief that the names Iberia and Hibernia (Ireland) were related, and that Ireland had been colonized from Spain. In fact, Celtic peoples lived in both lands and may conceivably have had direct contacts with each other.

The Milesians came for two reasons. The first was to avenge the death of Ith, Mil's grandfather, who had sailed to Ireland from Spain but had been killed with all his party. The second was that their druids had told them to invade: Ireland was their destiny. Mil led the party but died en route, leaving his wife Scota, the mythical ancestor of the Scots – a term that once referred to all Gaels, whether Irish or Scottish – and their eight sons. The leading son was the druid Amergin, who decided most matters of importance. The land to which they eventually came was at that time ruled by three grandsons of the Dagda and their wives Banbha, Fodla and Eriu, goddesses of sovereignty who were each said to have given their name to Ireland at some time or other (Eriu is the equivalent of modern Irish *Eire*). All three ruling families were arguing over how to divide the land, when the Milesians landed at the mouth of the Boyne. They arrived at Tara and demanded that the Dananns deliver up the island.

After a battle in which all three kings died, a compromise was reached: the Milesians would rule the upper half of the world and the Dananns would rule the Otherworld, the parallel universe below the visible world. The Dananns went to live in the *sidhe* or fairy mounds that marked the entrances to their new kingdom. Ireland was left in the hands of the Milesians and their descendants: the Gaels.

# The Ulster Wars

In the Ulster Cycle, Irish myth moves to the world of mortal superheroes. The action centres on the disputes between the kingdom of Ulster and Queen Maeve of Connacht and her allies. The cycle comprises many texts, but its essence is encapsulated in the *Tain Bo Cuailgne* ("The Cattle Raid of Cooley") in which an attempt to steal Ulster's prize bull is defeated almost singlehandedly by the hero Cuchulainn.

The Ulster Cycle presents a fascinating picture of ancient Celtic society. The characters are nominally Christian, but their ways are largely untainted by alien cultures – here are Rome's "barbarians" portrayed in all their gaudy, bloodstained splendour, fighting, drinking, womanizing and going into fits of battle-madness. These stories highlight the matriarchal nature of Celtic society: the power of women is often presented not only as equal to that of men but, as in the case of Maeve, exceeding it. The tales also reflect the directness which the Romans found so disturbing in the Celts. Sex, bloodshed and even defecation are described with relish. In one episode of the *Tain*, Cuchulainn beats his opponent so furiously that both are enclosed in a cloud of the man's excrement; thereafter, the text adds gleefully, his bowels were never quite the same.

Whether any of the characters really existed is doubtful. The topography, however, is authentic and it is possible to follow the progress of *The Cattle Raid of Cooley* on a map of Ireland. The spirit of place was very important to the Celts – the twelfth-century *Dinnshenchas* ("History of Places") gathers together much of the Irish lore on the subject – and the *Tain* is heavily laden with tales of how various physical features got their names.

The story begins in the time of Fergus mac Roich, mythical king of Ulster and, legend has it, author of the *Tain*. Fergus was a giant in every sense of the word. He had the strength of seven hundred men and he could consume at one sitting seven deer, seven pigs, seven cows and seven vats of alcohol. It took seven women to satisfy his rampaging sexual appetite. In battle he wielded a sword that was as long as a rainbow.

*Above*: **Navan Fort in County Armagh, the Emhain Macha of the Ulster myths. It was the capital of the historical kings of Ulster.**

Fergus desired his brother's widow, Nessa, who said she would marry him on condition that her son, Conchobar (Conor), be king of Ulster for a year. Fergus agreed, but Conchobar proved so popular that when the year was up the people of Ulster refused to have Fergus back. He was not too unhappy, however, being glad of the free time to go hunting, and so Conchobar remained king.

Under Conchobar, Ulster was a powerful province, famed for its warriors. The royal armies included the élite Red Branch and a youth brigade, a specially trained army of child warriors. At the forefront of the military stood Fergus and two other superheroes, Conall Cernach and Cuchulainn.

These last two were grandsons of the druid Cathbad, the king's chief adviser. But despite this strength, Ulster was overcome by a weakness that even Conchobar was unable to remedy.

It originated with Macha, a divine queen who had once been married to Nemed, one of Ireland's original invaders. Appearing in human guise, she married an Ulsterman, Crunnchru, and became pregnant with twins. Shortly before the birth her husband bragged that Macha could outrun the king's fastest horses. Conchobar immediately summoned her to a race at his capital and ignored all her pleas for the event to be put off until after she had given birth. And so Macha raced the horses and

# Deirdre of the Sorrows

*The story of Deirdre and Naoise (see picture, right) occurs in a manuscript dating from the ninth century. It was added to* **The Cattle Raid of Cooley** *to explain why Fergus supported Connacht in the raid rather than his native Ulster.*

Deirdre was the daughter of Fedlimid, Conchobar's chief storyteller. The druid Cathbad predicted that she would be the most beautiful woman in Ireland but that she would also cause many Ulster warriors to die. The men of Ulster wanted to kill the child at once, but Conchobar intended to marry her and hid her away with only a nurse for company.

One winter's day, when she was at the age to marry, Deirdre saw a raven drinking the blood of a slaughtered calf. "I could love a man with hair like the raven, cheeks like blood and skin like snow," she said. "There is such a man," the nurse said, "Naoise, son of Usna." One night, Deirdre went to meet Naoise, and they eloped to Scotland with two of his brothers. Word of this seeped back to Ulster. Conchobar was furious, but sent a peace offer to the sons of Usna. They agreed to return if Fergus accompanied them as surety for their safety. Conchobar agreed, but had Fergus delayed on a pretext, so Deirdre, Naoise and Naoise's brothers arrived at Emhain Macha without him. Conchobar at once asked one of his followers, Eoghan, to kill everyone except Deirdre. Naoise, his brothers and Fiacha, a son of Fergus, were all slaughtered. When Fergus learned of this treachery he left Ulster and offered his services to the queen of Connacht. Deirdre lived with Conchobar for a year but in the end her grief was so deep that it drove her to suicide: she hurled herself from a chariot and split her head on a stone. Her sorrows were at an end. As the druid had prophesied, those of Ulster were about to begin.

beat them, but as she crossed the finishing line she died, giving birth to twins at the same time. From this event was said to come the name of Conchobar's capital, Emhain Macha ("Twins of Macha"), present-day Fort Navan. With her last breath Macha cursed the men of Ulster: whenever the kingdom was threatened they would be afflicted for five days with unbearable pangs, as agonizing as those of childbirth. The curse would last for nine generations and the only people exempt were women, children and, perhaps because he was considered of partly divine origin, Cuchulainn.

Conchobar may have been an able ruler but, as the story of Macha shows, he also had an unpleasant streak. This trait was to initiate a damaging divide within the kingdom. The flashpoint was his love for the beautiful Deirdre, who eloped with another man (see page 57). To get her back, Conchobar resorted to methods that outraged Fergus's sense of honour and left his son Fiacha dead. Fergus consequently deserted to the neighbouring rival kingdom of Connacht, taking with him three thousand of Ulster's best warriors. This switch of allegiances brought about the deaths of many Ulster warriors in a great conflict between Conchobar's kingdom and the formidable Queen Maeve of Connacht.

## The Jealousy of Maeve

The war between Ulster and Connacht centred on two bulls of supernatural power: the White Horned Bull of Ai and the Brown Bull of Cooley. Famed for their size and strength, these animals were purportedly sent to Ireland by the gods in a deliberate attempt to incite war and bitterness. If so, the gods' purpose was amply fulfilled.

It all started with some idle pillow talk. As Ailill, the king of Connacht, lay in bed with his wife, Maeve, they began arguing over who was the wealthier. Ailill won by a narrow margin, citing his bull, Finnbhennach Ai, the White Horned Bull of Ai, the like of which was to be found nowhere else. Maeve was determined to equal the score and eventually learned of Donn Cuailgne, the Brown Bull of Cooley. Cooley, however, was in Ulster, beyond her jurisdiction, and the bull's owner did not want to part with it. Maeve therefore decided to take it by force and summoned to her aid not only the men of Connacht but also warriors from all the other provinces of Ireland except Ulster.

In origin Maeve was probably a goddess of fertility and sovereignty. She was a formidable woman – a strong leader and brave fighter with a ravenous sexual appetite. Even Fergus, who became her lover after his defection from Ulster,

Two bulls confront each other on this 2nd-century BC silver-plated iron torque found in southern Germany. Weighing some 6.5 kilograms, it was no doubt made as a votive offering to a god rather than as something to be worn.

# The Life of Cuchulainn

*Of all the Ulster champions none was more illustrious than Cuchulainn. With his divine connections, supernatural powers, magical weapons and short but brilliant life, he was the epic hero par excellence. His mother, Dechtire, was the daughter of the druid Cathbad. His father's identity, however, was a mystery, although in one story he was the god Lugh, the hero of the Dananns.*

Lugh is said to have made Dechtire pregnant in a dream while she was staying with King Conchobar and his hunting party by the river Boyne. Her child was named Setanta, but became known as Cuchulainn ("Hound of Culann") at a young age, after he had killed the fierce watchdog of Culann the smith and had taken its place until Culann had reared a new one. As a boy, he routed Conchobar's youth brigade and entered the Ulster king's service. He was trained in arms in Scotland by a female warrior, Scathach, who taught him such heroic feats as standing on a lance in flight and also gave him a vicious weapon called the *gae bolg*. A sort of spear, when it struck home its head sprouted thirty darts that coursed through every part of the victim's body, killing him instantly.

When his blood was up, Cuchulainn was gripped by a terrifying battle-frenzy during which his hair stood on end, his muscles bulged and his body rotated within its skin. One eye protruded from his head, the other sank into his skull and his battle-cry drove people insane.

*Cuchulainn in his battle-fury, wielding the* gae bolg, *his personal lethal weapon.*

He had many lovers, but always returned to his wife Emer. Cuchulainn appears in many Ulster Cycle tales, most notably *The Cattle Raid of Cooley*. His death came seven years after the raid, when Maeve plotted to kill him with six sorcerers, the children of Calatin, a druid slain by Cuchulainn. King Conchobar knew that not even a superhero could combat such an array of magic power, and tried to keep the warrior out of harm's way. But the sorcerers conjured up an illusion of battle which convinced Cuchulainn that Ulster was being laid waste. As he rode forth from his place of safety, he was struck by a magic spear thrown by one of the sorcerers. Mortally wounded, he tied himself to a rock so that he would be able to face his enemies with honour, standing up. For three days none of them dared approach him. In the end a war goddess, Badb, landed on his shoulder in the form of a crow. Cuchulainn did not stir, and so everyone knew that Ulster's greatest hero was dead.

was no match for her: on one tryst he lost his sword, a piece of symbolism which gave his fellows much amusement. Maeve was single-minded and selfish – the only reason she married Ailill was that he was financially generous and turned a blind eye to her love affairs. She was a born intriguer, happy to use deceit and trickery to achieve her ends.

Having determined to seize the Brown Bull, Maeve sent spies into Ulster. The report they brought back filled her with joy: every Ulster warrior except one was stricken by a mysterious complaint – the curse of Macha – and would offer no resistance. With Fergus to guide them, her armies set out in the direction of Cooley on the Monday after the feast of Samhain.

Fergus, however, was troubled at the thought of fighting the hero Cuchulainn, the only Ulster warrior unafflicted by the curse, and an old friend. He sent Cuchulainn a warning, and when the Connachtmen reached the Ulster border they found their way barred by a wooden hoop in which was carved a challenge in ogham script. Cuchulainn had

made the hoop from a living oak while standing on one leg and using one arm and one eye. The inscription challenged every invading warrior not to pass, on pain of dishonour, until he had made a hoop in the same way. "I except, of course, my friend Fergus," he added, and signed his name.

None could match Cuchulainn's achievement and so the army made a detour, only to be met by another impossible challenge. And so the delaying tactics continued, until eventually Maeve ordered her army simply to ignore them and advance. Cuchulainn then fell upon her men, killing them first in twos and threes, then, as he grew angrier, by the hundred. The mere sight of Cuchulainn in his battle-frenzy was enough to make seasoned warriors die of shock.

Finally, through Fergus's mediation, a compromise was reached whereby Cuchulainn's slaughter and Connacht's advance could both be slowed down. Cuchulainn promised not to lay into the Connacht troops, provided that he was met every day in single combat at a certain ford. While the

# Bricriu the Trickster

*Tricksters – subversive and often hilarious characters who tend to get their come-uppance – appear in many cultures. In Irish myth, the most notable trickster is Bricriu, a bard with the nickname "Poison Tongue".*

Bricriu was an archetypal mischief-maker who featured in many of the Ulster tales. Sometimes his cunning was helpful to Ulster; more often it was not. Yet his malevolence rarely caused serious damage and was usually humorous. In one episode, Bricriu tried to foment civil strife in Ulster by making three great warriors, including Cuchulainn, quarrel over who should receive the champion's portion – the greatest serving of food at a royal banquet, together with the privilege of sitting on the king's right hand.

To achieve this end, Bricriu invited the court to a great feast at his grand dwelling, threatening various calamities if they refused. The king and his men ignored his threats, however, until he finally swore that if they did not come he would make the breasts of their womenfolk beat together until they were black and blue. This did the trick, and the court, including the three heroes, headed for Bricriu's house. Once there, he provoked the quarrel, which turned into an almighty brawl that left his house a ruin. Bricriu ended up in a rubbish tip and emerged so filthy that nobody recognized him.

Bricriu met his end when he stepped in to judge between the Brown Bull of Ulster and the White Bull of Connacht. Ignoring his presence, the two bulls trampled him to death.

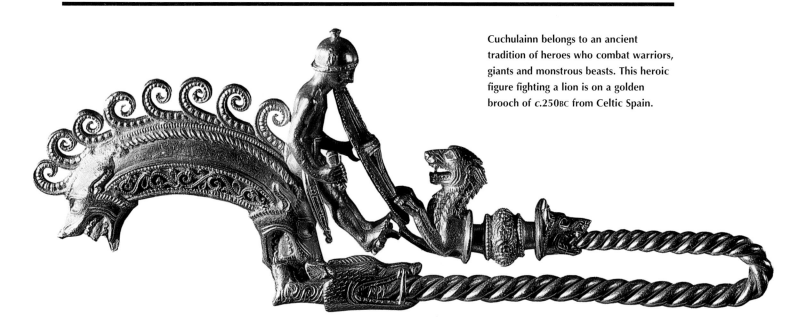

Cuchulainn belongs to an ancient tradition of heroes who combat warriors, giants and monstrous beasts. This heroic figure fighting a lion is on a golden brooch of *c.*250BC from Celtic Spain.

fight was taking place, Maeve and her troops were permitted to advance, but as soon as it had ended she had to call a halt for the day. "Better to lose one man a day than a hundred," said Maeve, confident that even if Cuchulainn could not be killed she would be able to find enough champions to keep him busy until her armies reached their destination.

At first plenty of heroes were willing to try their luck. But as each challenger was rapidly dispatched, Maeve had to offer increasingly large bribes to the others. Royal treasuries, herds of cattle, acres of land, the hand of Maeve's daughter – even the "friendly thighs" of Maeve herself – were promised. But no man who accepted a bribe lived to receive it. At one point Maeve managed to trick Fergus himself into meeting Cuchulainn. But the two had sworn that they would never fight each other. Instead, Cuchulainn pretended to run away, having first extracted a promise from Fergus that he would repay the favour on demand.

Finally, Maeve sent against Cuchulainn a great champion, Natchrantal, and although he died just like the others, he put up a strong enough fight for Maeve to be able to launch a lightning raid and bring the Brown Bull back to Connacht.

The raid should have stopped there, but Maeve continued to send men against Cuchulainn, among them another great champion, Ferdia. Until now, Cuchulainn had killed each of his challengers with a clear conscience. Ferdia, however, was his best friend. He had received the same training as Cuchulainn and was just as adept. The only thing he lacked was the secret weapon which had been given to no one except Cuchulainn: the *gae bolg,* an invariably lethal spear which, on entering its victim, sent tiny darts into every part of the body.

For three days the two heroes fought, with neither gaining the advantage, until on the fourth day, Cuchulainn was seized by his battle-frenzy and killed Ferdia with the *gae bolg.* In doing so, however, Cuchulainn himself was severely wounded. For several days he lay unable to move, and during this time the Ulstermen recovered from Macha's curse and joined battle with Maeve's army on the Plain of Garach. For a while it seemed as if the Connachtmen might win the day. Whole ranks fell at each swing of Fergus's sword. At one point Conchobar was at his mercy, but at the pleading of the king's sons Fergus diverted his stroke and lopped the tops off three nearby mountains.

The sound of battle reached Cuchulainn on his sickbed. When told that it was caused by Fergus's battle-fury, he rushed to the fray and demanded that Fergus return Cuchulainn's earlier favour by running away from him. Fergus fulfilled his part of the deal and took his supporters with him. Maeve

61

was left with only her own troops. The tide of battle turned, and Maeve's forces were put to flight. Maeve herself escaped death only because Cuchulainn considered it beneath himself to kill her.

Ironically, while all this blood was being shed, the two bulls were sorting out for themselves the issue of which was superior. On reaching Connacht the Brown Bull of Cooley challenged the White Horned Bull of Ai with three mighty bellows. All day and all night they fought, in a gargantuan contest that took them all over Ireland. By morning the white bull was dead and its victorious opponent made its way back to Ulster, scattering fragments of its foe around the countryside. As it reached the Ulster border, however, the exhausted animal died in an explosion of black vomit.

Many Irishmen had died – for absolutely nothing. The last word was left to Maeve. "We have had shame and shambles here today," she said. Nobody was inclined to disagree.

# Finn and the Fianna

Of the many heroes who inhabit Irish myth, Finn mac Cumhaill, anglicized as Finn MacCool, is perhaps the most celebrated. The adventures of Finn and his followers, the Fianna ("Warriors") or Fenians, form a great body of myth known as the Fenian Cycle, which was widely influential both in Ireland and beyond.

The stories of the Fianna spread to the Isle of Man and Scotland, where Finn is sometimes known in English as Fingal. The Fenian Cycle has also been credited as the source of certain Arthurian legends. The tale of Diarmaid and Grainne, for example, may be the origin of the story of Tristan and Isolde.

Finn was portrayed as a historical character in Irish literature and was said to have lived in the mid-third century AD. However, it is likely that he had already existed in oral tradition for many centuries and that his origins lay in ancient Celtic mythology. His upbringing and initial rise to fame bear a striking resemblance to those of Lugh, the god who saved the Tuatha De Danann from the monstrous Fomorians (see page 55). Finn means "fair" or "white" and Lugh means "bright" or "shining", so they may both be derived from a single Celtic deity, for example the god Lugus. Finn's mother, Muirne, certainly had divine blood in her veins, being descended from both Nuadu, king of the Tuatha De Danann, and Nuadu's enemy, Balor

A member of a band of Celtic warriors taking part in a raid against the Romans, part of a Roman frieze of c.175BC from Civitalba in Italy. Finn's warband was often called upon to attack the foreign enemies of the High King.

of the Evil Eye, leader of the Fomorians. (Lugh, too, was descended from both Balor and the Dananns.) Finn's father, Cumhall, was the leader of the Fianna, an élite band of the best Irish warriors who served as bodyguard to the High King of Ireland. It was the Fianna's job to protect Ireland from bandits and any danger from overseas. On one occasion, they defeated a foreign force led by a ruler known as the "High King of the Great World".

Shortly after Finn's birth, Cumhall was killed by a rival group, the sons of Morna, who coveted his position at the head of the Fianna. To protect her son from his father's enemies, Muirne spirited

# Finn and the Salmon of Knowledge

*The turning-point in Finn's life came at the age of seven when, under the pseudonym Deimne, he apprenticed himself to a bard called Finnegas to learn poetry. Finnegas lived on the banks of the river Boyne, where he tried to catch a salmon imbued with universal wisdom. Salmon symbolized knowledge and wisdom in Celtic tradition, perhaps because of their ability to find their way every year from the sea to spawning grounds many miles upriver.*

Around a well at the source of the Boyne there were nine hazel trees, on which grew nuts that held great wisdom. The nuts had fallen into the river and been eaten by a salmon. Thereafter, the first person to eat the flesh of the salmon would know all that there was to know. It had been prophesied that Finnegas would catch the fish.

For some seven years Finnegas fished for the salmon, but caught nothing. Shortly after Finn's arrival, however, Finnegas landed the salmon and asked Finn to clean and cook it. At the same time, he told Finn that on no account was he to eat even the tiniest bit of the fish, because the first to taste the fish would receive its magic. The boy was careful to obey his master in every respect. While the salmon was

**A salmon as depicted in the Book of Kells. Here it is linked with divine wisdom: a fish was a symbol of Christ for the early Christians.**

cooking, a blister arose on its skin. To burst it, Finn poked it with his thumb, but in doing so scalded himself. He sucked his thumb to ease the pain – and tasted the flesh of the magic salmon.

"What is your name?" asked Finnegas when he learned of this.

"Deimne," replied Finn, using the name he had taken to evade the sons of Morna. "No, it is not," said the bard. "It was foretold that I would catch the fish, but that Finn mac Cumhaill would be the first to eat it. You are he."

Finn ate the rest of the salmon and received the full power of prophecy. Whenever he wanted to use his gift, all he had to do was suck his thumb.

**A drawing based on a medieval Irish stone cross: the top panels are believed to show Finn sucking his thumb.**

Finn away to the forest of Slieve Bloom (in present-day County Laois) and entrusted his upbringing to two foster mothers, one of whom was a druid. Under their tutelage Finn learned the basic skills of the Irish warrior hero, such as running, leaping, swimming and hunting. In due course the young Finn left the forest and struck out on his own. From the king of Kerry, who had married his widowed mother, Finn learned of his ancestry. In Connacht he had his first taste of bloodshed when he killed a warrior involved in Cumhall's death. From the bard Finnegas, who lived by the banks of the Boyne, he learned the art of poetry.

Thus far, Finn had acquired all the attributes of a hero. But he was no mere mortal. Everything about him was endowed with supernatural significance: his ancestry; his upbringing at the hands of a druid;

and his childhood spent in natural surroundings. In addition, at the age of seven he had acquired prophetic omniscience from the Salmon of Knowledge. Finn was, in fact, something close to a god.

Eventually Finn presented himself to the High King of Ireland, Cormac mac Art, at the royal seat of Tara (in present-day County Meath) to offer his services. Finn did so on the eve of Samhain, a night when Ireland's erstwhile divine rulers, the Tuatha De Danann, emerged from their Otherworld kingdom to stalk the land. Every Samhain for the past nine years, Tara had been plagued by a Danann called Aillen. He would emerge from his fairy mound and lull everyone to sleep with his magic harp and pipes. Then, when all were slumbering, he would breathe flames from his mouth until Tara was burned to the ground. As Samhain approached, the High King asked if anyone could save Tara from destruction. Finn stepped forward and promised to guard Tara until the following dawn in return for anything he requested. The king agreed. Among the king's followers was a warrior named

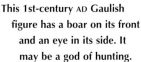

This 1st-century AD Gaulish figure has a boar on its front and an eye in its side. It may be a god of hunting.

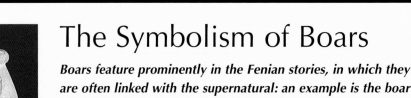

# The Symbolism of Boars

*Boars feature prominently in the Fenian stories, in which they are often linked with the supernatural: an example is the boar that killed the hero Diarmaid. From early times these fierce animals were of great symbolic significance to the Celts.*

Bronze boars have been found all over the Celtic world. Boars also appear on coins, and one panel of the Gundestrupp cauldron shows boar-shaped helmet crests. These beasts were probably symbols of royalty and military prowess, especially when depicted with bristles raised, a characteristic of a charging boar. There is evidence that boars were ritually sacrificed, perhaps as

offerings to hunting deities. Boars were often the central dish of warrior banquets and could thus symbolize feasting and hospitality as well as war and hunting: all these themes occur in the story of Finn and the boar-headed beast (see page 66). Numerous myths feature monstrous boars – for example, Twrch Trwyth in the Welsh tale of Culhwch and Olwen (see page 95).

Fiacha, who had been a close friend of Finn's father Cumhall. Fiacha gave Finn a magic spear which never missed its target and whose tip, when pressed to the forehead, would render Aillen's music ineffective.

Shortly after sunset, Aillen appeared. He played his harp and pipes and the guards of Tara fell into a deep sleep. Finn, however, pressed the spear tip to his forehead and stayed awake. As the first gust of flame billowed from Aillen's mouth, Finn caught the fire in his cloak and sent it into the earth. Again Aillen breathed flame and again it was driven underground. Aillen realized that he had met a magic greater than his own, and started to run for home. But no matter how fast he ran, Finn was able to keep up with him. Just as Aillen reached the door of his fairy mound, Finn ran him through with the magic spear with such force that his heart burst from his mouth. Finn cut off Aillen's head and returned to Tara, where he stuck the head on a pole and laid beside it the magic harp and pipes. Then he sat beside his trophies and waited for sunrise, when everyone woke up and acclaimed his deed.

The High King was honour-bound to reward Finn with whatever the hero requested. Finn demanded the leadership of the Fianna – a post currently occupied by Goll, one of his father's killers. (This is another link with the Lugh story: Goll means "One-Eyed", and Lugh's enemy was Balor, the one-eyed Fomorian king.) However, Goll generously agreed to step down in favour of Finn and thereafter the two became firm friends.

## The Fianna under Finn

Under Finn, the Fianna numbered over twenty thousand men with seven hundred and fifty chiefs, each of whom commanded a force of twenty-seven warriors. They were a tough bunch. A prospective member had to be able to jump over a stick his own height, duck under another at knee level, and remove a thorn from his foot with one fingernail – all while running as fast as possible. The Fianna warrior swore four things: never to take cattle by force; never to refuse a request for money; never to retreat if outnumbered less than ten to one; and never to avenge any harm done to his kinsmen. The Fianna man had to renounce family and home for a military life in which, however, he lacked for nothing. The Fianna had their own druids, doctors, poets and musicians, as well as fifty women who did nothing but make clothes for them. They also received excellent pay from the people of Ireland.

Finn had a number of supernatural helpers. One was "Little Nut", a Danann bard who stood only four feet high, but played music more beauti-

When they were not fighting or hunting, the Fianna spent much of their time feasting. This scene from a feast is from a bronze vessel found in a 5th-century BC Celtic tomb in northern Italy.

fully than anyone and could remember every story ever told. Finn also had two hounds, Bran and Sceolan, born to Finn's sister while she had been temporarily transformed into a dog by a goddess. A woman called Sadb, who had been changed into a deer for refusing the love of a druid, was captured by the Fianna, whereupon she turned back into a human and became Finn's wife. Their son Oisin ("Little Fawn") grew to become almost as great a hero as Finn. Oisin's own son, Oscar, led a Fianna troop known as "The Terrible Broom" from its ability to sweep the enemy off the field.

The Fianna's frequent hunting expeditions emphasized Finn's closeness to both the natural and supernatural realms. On one hunt, in Leinster, Finn's party met a curious animal with long horns, a boar's head, a deer's body and an image of the moon on each flank. Behind it walked a mysterious red woman. The woman and the beast led the Fianna through a fairy mound into the Otherworld, where they entered a great hall in which a Danann king was holding a feast. He welcomed Finn and his men and showed them the creature they had been chasing. In a voice like a man's, the beast boasted of its speed – then fled out of the mound with the entire company, Danann and human alike, in pursuit. Bran finally brought the animal down, whereupon the red woman declared that the beast had once been a king of the Firbolgs, the former rulers of Ireland. His death, she prophesied ominously, spelled trouble for the island in times to come.

As Finn grew older, younger men began to challenge his power. His less pleasant characteristics now came to the fore – like Conchobar in the Ulster Cycle, Finn had a cruel streak. Nowhere was this more evident than in his quarrel with the warrior Diarmaid Ua Duibhne.

## Diarmaid and Grainne

Diarmaid Ua Duibhne had no divine blood, but his foster father was the god Oenghus (see page 69), and he was raised at Oenghus's home at Newgrange on the Boyne. Diarmaid became one of the most famous members of the Fianna. On one early adventure, he encountered a supernatural woman who touched his brow with her finger, leaving a "love-spot" that made him irresistible to women.

Finn was an ageing warrior when he decided to take a wife, and his choice fell on Grainne, the High King's daughter. At the betrothal feast, however, Grainne saw Diarmaid's love-spot and fell in love with him at once. She drugged the other guests with a sleeping potion, then imposed on Diarmaid a geis, a request that could not be refused without the loss of all honour: in the Irish heroic code, anyone could impose a geis on a warrior at any time. Grainne's geis was that Diarmaid should elope with her. Faced with disgrace if he refused and the wrath of Finn if he agreed, Diarmaid consented, but insisted that he would not be her lover.

When Finn discovered what had happened, he flew into a rage and began to pursue the couple obsessively. For sixteen years the leader of the

**Diarmaid fights Searbhan the giant. During their flight from Finn, Diarmaid and Grainne encountered a one-eyed giant, Searbhan ("Surly"), who guarded a magic tree in the forest of Dubhnos. At first Diarmaid befriended the normally dangerous Searbhan, who helped the couple to hide from Finn. But when Grainne asked to eat the fruit of the tree, Searbhan grew angry and got into a fight with Diarmaid, who killed him.**

# Giants

*The giants that appear in many Celtic myths are not always the evil ogres of folklore, although some, such as the one-eyed Searbhan, Balor (see page 54) and Ysbaddaden (see page 92) come close to this category.*

**The Celtic giant cut into the chalk downs at Cerne Abbas in Dorset has been dated to the early Roman period. Recent research has suggested a link with the superhuman Classical hero Hercules, whom the Celts associated with various deities of their own.**

Some giants may be linked to ancient pagan deities, their former divine status hinted at in their superhuman size. For example, Searbhan and the Green Knight of Arthurian legend (see page 114), are both associated with forests, like the old god Cernunnos. In many cases it is not easy to determine whether the term "giant" is used literally, or in a figurative sense to mean someone of great prowess or supernatural gifts. Evidently, however, the literal and metaphorical senses were to a certain degree inextricable, so that great warriors such as Fergus and Cuchulainn were portrayed as also being of huge size. Later tales of Finn refer to him as a giant, and he appears as such in Gaelic folklore: he was said to have built the "Giants' Causeway" linking Ireland to Scotland. Folktales about King Arthur, too, describe him as a person of gigantic physical stature. Like the Greek Cyclopes, the malevolent giants of Celtic myth often have only one eye. This feature may derive from the widespread ancient concept of the "evil eye".

Fianna was occupied in the pursuit, in which time Ireland was reduced to near-anarchy. Finn used his magic powers of insight to find where the couple were, but each time Oenghus intervened to save them. To make matters worse, Grainne eventually persuaded Diarmaid to become her lover.

Finally, Finn tracked the runaways down to Oenghus's house at Newgrange on the Boyne. When Oenghus proposed a truce, Finn and Diarmaid agreed. Diarmaid was at last welcomed as the king's son-in-law, and Finn was given another of the High King's daughters in compensation.

But Finn never forgave Diarmaid. He organized a hunt for a great boar that lived on the slopes of Ben Bulben in Sligo. This boar had started life as the illegitimate child of Diarmaid's mother and Oenghus's steward, Roc. Oenghus's father killed the boy, but Roc brought him back to life as a boar with no hair, ears or tail. He also uttered a curse: one day the boar would kill Diarmaid.

The hero knew nothing of his monstrous half-brother until he received an invitation to the boar hunt from Finn. When Diarmaid arrived, Finn told him the boar's history and Diarmaid realized that he had been lured into a trap. He was resigned to his fate. "If it is here I am to find my death, then so be it," he declared. He lunged at the boar, which disembowelled him even as he dealt it a fatal blow.

As he lay dying, Diarmaid begged Finn to cure him, which he had the magic power to do simply by letting Diarmaid drink water from his hands. Three times Finn took water to Diarmaid, but each time he remembered his old grudge and allowed the water to trickle away through his fingers. And so Diarmaid died, and Oenghus took his foster son's body away for burial at Newgrange.

A rider and his hound pursue a boar on this 2nd-century BC bronze cult wagon from Celtic Spain. On their hunting expeditions, Finn and the Fianna often pursued magic boars that led them into the Otherworld.

## The End of the Fianna

Diarmaid's death revealed the dark side of Finn, who had previously been seen as the perfect hero. As his character deteriorated, so did the status and behaviour of the Fianna. They grew increasingly aloof from normal society and the payment previously given freely by the Irish people became a tribute which the Fianna demanded. Such arrogance inevitably led to a confrontation with the High King of Ireland. When a marriage was arranged for one of the High King's daughters, the Fianna demanded a huge cut of the dowry. The sovereign refused and summoned the Irish provincial kings to his court. "I would sooner die fighting the Fianna," he announced, "than live in Ireland under them as it is now."

Ireland was split by the challenge. The clan of Morna, which had hitherto supported Finn, defected to the High King, while the king of Munster sided with the Fianna. In the ensuing battle of Gawhra, the bloodshed was immense. It was said that only old men and boys were left alive in Ireland afterwards. Finn's grandson Oscar killed the High King, but was himself mortally wounded. His death heralded the Fianna's downfall. Oisin disappeared with a princess from the Otherworld (see page 30) and one by one the Fianna passed away. One account tells how a band of twenty-seven Fianna once travelled to Tara. "They saw that now they lacked their full strength and great name, no one took notice of them or spoke to them. When they saw this, they lay down on the side of the hill at Tara, put their lips to the earth, and died."

As for Finn, his precise fate was uncertain. In one account, he was so dishonoured by contriving Diarmaid's death that the Fianna abandoned him: he later died while trying to leap the Boyne. But other stories parallel Arthurian legend: Finn did not die, but sleeps with his remaining warriors in a cave, where they will one day awake to save Ireland in its hour of need.

# Oenghus, God of Love

Love played a prominent part in Irish myth. Often it was a force for good, a symbol of universal harmony and prosperity. Sometimes, however, it sparked quarrels which had a debilitating effect on the land, as in the stories of Deirdre and Diarmaid. It was Oenghus's job to ensure that the course of love ran smoothly.

Oenghus was the offspring of the Dagda and Boann, the goddess of the river Boyne. He was also known as Mac Oc, or "Young Son", a name that links him with the British deity Maponus ("Son"), the Welsh Mabon. Maponus may have been a god of music and poetry, perhaps love poetry in particular. Oenghus's home was said to be the ancient passage grave of Newgrange on the Boyne, where Oenghus kept the body of Diarmaid after his death. Whenever Oenghus wanted to talk with Diarmaid, he could breathe a temporary soul into the corpse.

Oenghus often intervened on behalf of lovers in peril: the story of Diarmaid and Grainne is the most famous such tale. Another tells how Midir,

Oenghus's brother, fell in love with the beautiful Etain. Midir's jealous wife, Fuamnach, turned her into a giant red fly, but Oenghus partly counteracted the spell and Etain became human again at night. One day, however, Fuamnach sent a wind that blew Etain into the wilderness, where she spent a thousand years before falling into a cup of wine as it was being drunk by an Ulster hero's wife. Etain was swallowed with the wine and was later reborn. When Midir at last found her, she had married the High King of Ireland. Midir tricked the king into letting him kiss the bride, who at once recalled her past life and fell in love with Midir again. They both turned into swans and flew away to his home.

**Scenes from the life of Oenghus. Left to right: Oenghus and his home at Newgrange – it was said that four birds hovered over his head at all times, a sign of his divinity; Etain turns into a red fly; she falls into a cup; she is reborn to the wife of an Ulster hero.**

# The Dream of Oenghus

*Oenghus himself was not immune to the effects of love. One story relates how, every night for a year, he dreamed of a beautiful woman. She would appear, beckon to him, then disappear as he reached out to her. Because of the dream, Oenghus grew pale and listless, and would not touch his food.*

Doctors were summoned but Oenghus was too embarassed to admit that he was in love with a dream. Finally, one of the best doctors of the Tuatha De Danann, Fergne, diagnosed his problem.

Oenghus's mother, the goddess Boann, was then called and given the task of searching Ireland for the woman Oenghus had seen in his dreams. She failed and Oenghus's father, the Dagda, was given the same task. He too was unsuccessful. Thereupon Boann's brother, Bobd Dearg, was enlisted to help. For a year he scoured the land and finally reported success. The woman was the daughter of a Danann god and lived by a lake in Connacht. Oenghus also learnt her name:

Caer. Oenghus went to speak to King Ailill and Queen Maeve of Connacht. The Dagda also intervened on his behalf, and Ailill summoned Caer's father, Ethal. He refused to come, however, so Ailill's warriors destroyed the fairy mound where the god lived. Even so, Ethal still refused to hand over his daughter. When questioned, he replied that she had powers greater than his: on every day of one year she appeared as a human, but on every day of the next year she took the shape of a bird. In the end Ethal conceded that if Oenghus really wanted her, he must arrange to be at the lake on the feast of Samhain of the following year.

Oenghus did as he was asked and found the lake covered with

**Oenghus beckons the swan-maiden Caer from the shore of the lake. He was able to recognize her from the necklace she was wearing.**

one hundred and fifty swans, among them Caer. He called to her from the shore but she said that she would only come if Oenghus allowed her to return to the water as a swan. Oenghus agreed and turned himself into a swan so that he could join her.

The couple embraced and swam round the lake three times, consummating their love as they did so. They then flew away to Oenghus's home at Newgrange. Once there, they regained human form and held a great feast, at which they both sang so beautifully that all their guests were lulled to sleep for three days and nights.

# Fantastic Journeys

A significant body of Irish mythological tales recount voyages to the Otherworld. These stories are distinct from others that involve incursions into the Otherworld by heroes – Finn, for example, occasionally crossed into it while hunting – in that their protagonists are usually ordinary people rather than great warriors. Many of the tales revolve around quests, such as the search for a kidnapped wife or the hunt for a murderer.

The Otherworld could be reached in many ways: through a hill, a lake or a mist. For voyagers, however, it consisted of a string of magical islands, far across the sea, which comprised the kingdom of Manannan, son of the sea god Lir. Manannan controlled the oceans around Ireland and was thus revered as one of the island's guardian deities. He was said to have been the first king of Man, and to have given his name to the island. In later myth, he was described as one of the Tuatha De Danann.

One voyager to the Otherworld was Tadg, son of Cian of Munster. Tadg's wife and two brothers had been seized in a raid by foreigners, so he mounted a retaliatory raid by sea. Tadg and his crew sailed through raging storms, until finally the waters grew calm and they found themselves on an island of great peace and beauty. They were amazed to find that it was summer there, although it had been winter in Ireland when they had set out.

Moreover, despite the hardships they had been through, they felt not the slightest hunger. Advancing further, they came to three hills. On each hill stood a fort: one was white, one gold and one silver. Approaching the white fort, they were greeted by a beautiful woman. Tadg enquired who lived there and was told it was the home of the Milesian

**A miniature ship, made in the 1st century BC in solid gold, complete with oars and mast. It was part of a hoard discovered at Broighter in County Derry.**

kings of Ireland. At the silver fort they met another beautiful woman to whom Tadg put the same question. It was home, he was told, to everyone else who had once ruled Ireland: Partholon, Nemed, the Firbolgs and the Tuatha De Danann. At the third hill, they learned that the golden fort was reserved for all the future kings of Ireland, and Tadg himself would find a place there one day. It turned out that the island's ruler was Cliodna, a Danann goddess of great beauty. When Tadg and his crew left for home, she sent three birds to guide them. En route

A silver plaque of c.75BC from central Europe. The three-swirl or triskele motif has been linked with water gods. The three-legged symbol of the Isle of Man, the realm of the sea god Manannan, is similar.

they defeated the raiders and came home with Tadg's wife and brothers and much booty.

Tadg was lucky, because trouble often came to those who chose to leave the Otherworld. Bran, son of Febal, sailed there but he and his crew grew homesick. They were allowed to see Ireland again on condition that they did not set foot on Irish soil. When their boat reached the coast, however, one of the crew leapt ashore. The moment his feet touched land, he disintegrated into a pile of ashes

# The Voyage of Mael Duin

*The tale of Mael Duin is the earliest known Celtic travel myth. It formed the basis of many others, such as* The Voyage of St Brendan, *one of the most popular stories of medieval Europe.*

Mael Duin was the son of a nun and a famous warrior, Ailill Edge-of-Battle. Before his birth, Ailill was killed in battle, and when Mael Duin grew to maturity he swore to avenge his father's death. A druid told him that the land where the killers lived could only be reached by sea, and that he must take no more than seventeen men with him. As Mael Duin sailed away, however, his three foster brothers jumped into the sea and begged him to take them. To save them from drowning, he took them aboard. After one day and half a night of hard rowing, they came to two small islands, the home of the men who had killed Ailill. Mael

Duin got ready to land, but a sudden tempest blew up and sent his boat far out to sea. "This is your fault," he berated his foster-brothers. "Because of you I have disobeyed the druid."

The storm continued, and eventually they strayed among the magic islands of the Otherworld. One was inhabited by giant ants, another by giant horses, a third by a beast that alternately revolved within its skin or had the skin revolve around its body. From the cliffs of one island, Mael Duin seized a twig that bore three magic apples, each of which fed the whole crew for forty days. On another, they gathered fruit in orchards tended by red, fiery pigs whose underground sties heated the whole island. When all the fruit had gone, they found another island on which stood a white tower, whose rooms, full of food and treasures, were guarded only by a cat. They ate their fill under its watchful gaze, but as they were leaving, one of Mael Duin's foster-brothers snatched a necklace from the wall. The cat at once leapt right through him and reduced him to cinders.

On the next island lived two flocks of sheep, one white and one black. They were divided by a wall, and guarded by a giant who would occasionally pick a sheep and put it on the other side of the wall, whereupon it changed colour. After this came an island full of black-coloured people weeping. When the second of Mael Duin's foster-brothers landed he too turned black and started to weep, and a rescue party could not bring him back.

With just one excess passenger aboard, Mael Duin and his crew sailed on. They encountered a bronze-doored fortress reached by a glass bridge; an island which had started as a sod of Irish soil but which each year grew a foot in breadth and sprouted a new tree; the Isle of Prophecy, whose inhabitants shouted, "It is they!" and pelted them with nuts; a huge silver column, from the top of which a giant trawled a silver net; and, finally, the Isle of Women, where Mael Duin and his men found wives and were promised eternal youth. Mael Duin married the island's queen.

After three months, the crew became homesick and demanded to leave. As they sailed away, the queen threw Mael Duin the end of a length of twine which stuck to his hand and allowed her to draw them back. Three months later they again tried to leave and the same thing happened. At the third attempt, realizing that Mael Duin secretly wanted to stay, a crewman cut off his hand as he caught the rope and the ship finally made its escape.

On they voyaged, past more strange islands, until they came to the Isle of the Laughing Folk, whose inhabitants lived in perpetual joy. They drew lots as to who was to land first and the third foster-brother won. He set foot on the island and immediately began laughing and singing along with the rest of the islanders. He could not be persuaded to leave, so Mael Duin left him and sailed away.

With no illicit crew members aboard, Mael Duin could now return home. A falcon led Mael Duin and his crew southeastwards back to Ireland, where they landed on the island of his father's killers. Mael Duin confronted the men he sought, but they greeted him like a hero after his long journey into the Otherworld. With no heart left for vengeance, Mael Duin recounted his extraordinary adventures.

# A PALACE FOR THE GODS

The pre-Celtic tombs that dot the Irish countryside were tailor-made for Gaelic myth. In Celtic eyes, each one became an enchanted mound or *sidh*, in which dwelled one of the gods and spirits of the Otherworld. No *sidh* commanded more reverence than the great passage grave at Newgrange in County Meath, which features in several myths: it was said to be the home of Oenghus, the god of love. Built some 5,200 years ago – before the Egyptian pyramids – it is part of a prehistoric cemetery complex on the River Boyne known as Brugh Na Boinne. Constructed as a gigantic cairn of river boulders, it encloses a narrow passage leading to a central burial chamber.

*Above*: Newgrange is made up of 450 huge boulders and over a million sackfuls of smaller stones. It could have taken 40 years to build – an average Stone Age lifetime.

*Right*: Dismissed in the 18th century as "barbarous", these spirals may represent the soul's journey from life to rebirth. Such motifs may have inspired Irish artists.

*Opposite*: The tomb's central chamber, where the love god Oenghus was said to reside (see page 69), is pierced by a single shaft of sunlight at dawn on midwinter's day. The chamber's unique corbelled roof prevents water seepage and spreads the huge weight of earth and rocks above.

# TALES OF MAGIC AND TRANSFORMATION

In Ireland, Celtic culture was unchallenged (except for Viking incursions) until the English invasions of the Middle Ages; in Wales, it had to co-exist with foreign influence, and sometimes alien rule, from Roman times. Even after the Romans had gone, other invaders came in their wake, of whom the most persistently hostile were the Anglo-Saxons from northern Germany. Slowly but steadily, the German newcomers pushed back the Britons to the western extremities of Britain.

Astonishingly, given their propensity for tribal squabbles, the Celts clung together. In the battle of Brunanburh, fought in AD937 at a still unidentified site, they even formed a coalition against their enemies. It was a huge force which included armies from Wales, Scotland, Cumbria, Cornwall, the Isle of Man, Ireland, and even some Norsemen who had settled around Dublin. But the coalition was defeated by the Anglo-Saxon king Athelstan, and from that time on the Britons were destined to face permanent English overlordship. Wales preserved its own identity, divided into three kingdoms – Gwynedd in the north, Dyfed in the south and Powys in the centre – until the last independent Welsh ruler died in 1282. Since that time the title "Prince of Wales" has been borne by the crown princes of England.

*Below*: A young sea deity riding a fish, from the 3rd-century BC Gundestrupp cauldron. In Welsh myth, the sea god Dylan swam "as well as the best fish" from the moment of his birth.

At the very time when their independence was under threat, Welsh bards made a determined effort to resurrect the past. Some of their material was Irish in origin, but as much or more came from British sources. The result, as recorded by later scribes, was the *Mabinogion*, a disparate collection of tales that lacks the cohesiveness of the Irish stories and veers in places towards the styles of medieval literature. Yet the *Mabinogion* also encompasses many themes inherited from the remote past, along with a fantastical quality that is unmistakably Celtic. At the heart of the collection are the Four Branches, which cover most of Wales and its neighbours. The First and Third branches are set in Dyfed, traditionally associated with mystery, and the Welsh Otherworld of Annwn. The Second and Fourth range from Gwynedd, the land of magic, to Ireland and England.

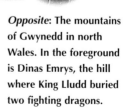

*Opposite*: The mountains of Gwynedd in north Wales. In the foreground is Dinas Emrys, the hill where King Lludd buried two fighting dragons.

77

# The Sources of Welsh Myth

There are three main sources for Welsh myth as we know it. First there are the semi-legendary works of clerical historians working in Latin, such as Nennius and Geoffrey of Monmouth. Secondly, there is Old French material drawing upon the Welsh and Breton bardic traditions, notably the works of Chrétien de Troyes and Marie de France. But the most significant source is the literature in Welsh and, in particular, the *Mabinogion*.

The oldest of the Welsh written texts is *Gododdin*, which according to tradition dates back to the sixth century AD. It is an account of a war in the land of Gododdin, the then British-speaking southeastern lowlands of Scotland. However, most surviving manuscripts of *Gododdin* date from the thirteenth to fifteenth centuries. From this period too come several important collections of tales, including *The White Book of Rhydderch* and *The Red Book of Hergest*. These contain the eleven tales known

PICTS
Edinburgh
GODODDIN
RHEGED
CUMBRIA
NORTHUMBRIA

**The Lands of Welsh Myth**

Anglesey  ARFON
MT. SNOWDON
GWYNEDD  • Chester
• Dinas Emrys
• Harlech

WALES  POWYS  Severn  LLOEGYR (ENGLAND)
Hereford  Gloucester
DYFED  Carmarthen
Gwales  Arberth  Monmouth  Oxford
PENVRO  London
(PEMBROKE)  Thames
DEVON
CORNWALL

since the nineteenth century as the *Mabinogion*: the "Four Branches"; *Culhwch and Olwen*; *The Dream of Macsen*; *Lludd and Llefelys*; *The Dream of Rhonabwy*; and three Arthurian romances, *The Lady of the Fountain*, *Peredur* and *Geraint and Enid* (the latter are covered in the next chapter). Some of the stories are recorded in earlier sources: the Four Branches, for example, were first collected and arranged into their current form in the eleventh century. As is the case with *Gododdin*, the language of the stories sometimes places them even further back in time. *Culhwch and Olwen*, for example, probably dates to before the year 1000.

The collections from which the *Mabinogion* come are supplemented by bardic sources. These include the *Triads of the Island of Britain*, summaries of longer tales arranged in thematic groups of three as an *aide-mémoire* for bards and minstrels. They were carried about from place to place by these wandering poets and scholars and survived only when recorded by others. The best-known of the bardic sources, however, relate to a celebrated bard called Taliesin, whose identification with Taliesin Ben Beird, a real poet of the sixth century in the service of the historical King Urien of Rheged, is a matter of debate. Twelve poems attributed to Taliesin have survived, along with the thirteenth-century *Book of Taliesin*, which contains tales from much earlier times, many of them extremely obscure.

The *Mabinogion* is the most important of the Welsh sources. However, it was largely unknown, even among the Welsh, until the nineteenth-century folklorist Lady Charlotte Guest translated a number of Welsh tales into English under this title, which

# The Birth of Taliesin

*Taliesin was to become the greatest of all the Welsh bards. Works attributed to him include* The Spoils of Annwn, *describing a visit by Arthur to the Otherworld, and the famous* Boast of Taliesin, *in which the poet – supposedly only thirteen years old at the time – laid claim to nothing less than omniscience. This legend, which has echoes of the Irish tale of Finn and the Salmon of Knowledge, describes how he first came by his great wisdom.*

The witch Ceridwen probably derives from the Great Hag, a type of formidable and sinister Celtic land goddess. Such a goddess may be depicted on this panel from the 3rd-century BC Gundestrupp cauldron, her powerful status indicated by the torque she wears around her neck.

To judge from the story, Taliesin's career began in the most unpromising manner. Afaggdu, "Utter Darkness", was indisputably the ugliest man in the world and all the magic powers of his mother, the witch Ceridwen, could not change that fact. However, Ceridwen decided that if Afaggdu was going to be ugly, he could at least be clever, and so she prepared a potion for him that would reveal all the mysteries of the universe.

It was not a simple process. The brew had to simmer for a year and a day, with herbs added at certain specified times. Towards the end of the year, as Ceridwen was gathering the last of the ingredients, a small boy called Gwion came and watched the boiling pot. As he did so, the mixture bubbled up and spat three drops onto his finger. He licked them off and immediately received the wisdom intended for Afaggdu.

When Ceridwen returned there was nothing Gwion could do to make amends. He had drunk the three most important drops in the cauldron and the rest was useless. He fled before her wrath, but try as he might he could not escape. He turned himself into a hare, she turned into a hound. He turned into a fish, she into an otter. When he became a bird, she became a hawk; finally, he turned into a grain of wheat, but Ceridwen changed into a hen and ate him.

On resuming her human form, Ceridwen found that she was pregnant, and in due course she gave birth to Gwion. But the reborn boy was so handsome that she could not bring herself to kill him, so she trussed him up in a leather bag and hurled him into the sea.

Two days later, however, on the first day of May, the bag was retrieved from the sea by Elphin, the nephew of Maelgwyn, king of Dyfed. Elphin gave the beautiful child a new name – Taliesin, "Shining Brow" – and fostered him as his own son.

79

strictly speaking applies only to the Four Branches. The translation, originally aimed at children, proved so popular that the *Mabinogion* remains the most famous of Welsh narrative collections to this day.

The *Mabinogion* is set against a background of real and recognizable places and includes historical characters alongside elements of magic, transformation, death and resurrection. Although they took on their present form in the Middle Ages, the stories in the *Mabinogion* contain many ancient Celtic themes, and Celtic gods appear in the Four

Branches. The Third Branch features the family of Llyr and Manawyddan, Welsh variants of the Irish Lir and his son Manannan. The *Mabinogion* also has Christian elements, for the Britons were converted in Roman times, and remained Christian while the Anglo-Saxons were still pagan. Clearly, many figures of Celtic myth made the transition to the new religion with their names and functions only slightly adapted. Several characters came out of ancient Welsh legend to join Arthur in his later, Christian quests for the Holy Grail.

# *The Lord of the Otherworld*

The First Branch of the *Mabinogion* concerns Pwyll, king of the southern region of Wales known as Dyfed. His name, meaning "Sense", has been linked to the "Lord of Great Knowledge", one of the titles given to Ireland's Dagda. Pwyll also has other supernatural connections: he becomes, briefly, king of the Welsh Otherworld of Annwn; his wife Rhiannon has similarities with Epona, the old Celtic horse goddess, and his son, Pryderi, is born in circumstances of typically divine mystery.

**A hound depicted on a 4th-century BC wine flagon from France. Fantastic dogs like Arawn's are associated with the Otherworld (see page 29).**

While out hunting, Pwyll saw a pack of hounds with white bodies and red ears pursuing a stag. He drove them off and set his own dogs on the stag, unwittingly offending Arawn, the king of Annwn, who owned the strange dogs. Arawn appeared and demanded that Pwyll should make amends. His wish was that the two should exchange places for a year, at the end of which Pwyll would have to fight a duel against Arawn's deadly rival, Hafgan. During the year, the two kings would also magically exchange appearances, so that none of their subjects would be any the wiser. When Pwyll accepted, Arawn gave him a piece of vital advice: Hafgan could only be killed by a single blow; two blows and he would instantly recover from his wounds.

The deal was struck, and Arawn led Pwyll to his new home. The magic worked. Everybody thought Pwyll was Arawn, even Arawn's wife. But Pwyll did not take advantage of the deception. In

# The House of Llyr

*Of the two dynasties which underpin the Mabinogion, that of Llyr is the focus of both the Second and Third Branches. Llyr was in origin a sea god, the Welsh equivalent of Ireland's Lir. He had two wives, the first being Iweriadd (Ireland) and the second Penardun, daughter of the goddess Don, whose offspring constitute the other great dynasty of Welsh mythology.*

The children of Llyr and Iweriadd included Bran the Blessed and his sister Branwen. From Llyr's marriage to Penardun came Manawyddan. Llyr found his way into a wider cultural context when he was incorporated into Geoffrey of Monmouth's *History of the Kings of Britain* as Leir, a mythical king of Britain. The plot of Shakespeare's tragedy *King Lear* ultimately derives from Geoffrey's account of how the king was dispossessed by two of his daughters. Unlike the Shakespearean version of the story, however, Geoffrey's has a happy ending, with the third daughter eventually restoring the deposed king to his throne. According to the *Mabinogion*, Llyr has only one daughter, Branwen. But she is described as one of "the three matriarchs of Britain" (the other two are not named), and this phrase may lie at the root of the tradition that King Lear had three female offspring.

**The family tree of Llyr.**

---

bed that night, and on every night for the rest of the year, he turned his face to the wall and neither touched nor spoke to the queen. After twelve months, Pwyll went to fight Hafgan. With his first blow he fatally wounded his opponent. Hafgan begged for a *coup-de-grâce* to put him out of his agony. But Pwyll refused to deliver the second blow which would have restored him, and so Hafgan perished.

When Arawn returned he was delighted to find that Pwyll had killed Hafgan and he joined the dead man's kingdom to his own. Pwyll was equally pleased with the way in which Arawn had governed Dyfed. In fact, the only disappointed person was Arawn's wife, who accused Arawn of neglecting her for a year. At that, Arawn was even more impressed with Pwyll. The two monarchs became firm friends, and from that time on Pwyll was known as "Lord of the Otherworld".

## Pwyll and Rhiannon

Outside Pwyll's court at Arberth was a mound. It was said that whoever sat on it would either be harmed or see an amazing thing. One day, Pwyll decided to put the claim to the test.

He sat down and after a little while saw a beautiful woman approaching on a white horse. He sent his men in pursuit but, although she seemed to move at a gentle pace, they found that they were unable to catch up with her.

The next day the woman came again, and this time Pwyll himself ran after her, begging her to stop. She did so, and explained to him that she was Rhiannon, daughter of Hefeydd Hen. She had been betrothed to a man called Gwawl against her will, and had fled to Pwyll in the hope that he would take her as his wife. Pwyll agreed at once, setting the wedding date for twelve months time. After a year, Pwyll presented himself at Hefeydd Hen's court, where a sumptuous banquet had been prepared. But as he was feasting a young man came up and asked him to grant a favour. Magnanimously, Pwyll offered to give him whatever he wished for. Only then did the man reveal that he was none other than Gwawl, Rhiannon's rejected suitor, and that what he wanted was Rhiannon herself.

Pwyll was honour-bound to keep his word. Rhiannon cursed him for his stupidity, but also took the opportunity to give him a magic bag which, she suggested, could be used to thwart Gwawl's plans for her. The following year another banquet was held, with Gwawl in Pwyll's place. Like Pwyll, he was in a generous mood when an old beggar entered the hall and asked for food to fill his bag. But the bag proved impossible to fill, and the beggar insisted it would remain so until some rich man got in and stamped down the contents. Gwawl volunteered, at which point the beggar – who was none other than Pwyll in disguise – closed the top of the bag and summoned his men, who were waiting outside. They then proceeded to kick the bag around the room until the helpless Gwawl pleaded for mercy. Pwyll granted it, but only after his bruised and battered rival had agreed to hand Rhiannon back to him.

A bronze horse head of *c.*75 AD from Yorkshire. Rhiannon's name probably derives from Rigantona, "Great Queen", and she has links with the horse goddess Epona.

# Pryderi

*Pryderi, the son of Pwyll and Rhiannon, was abducted shortly after his birth. Fearing for their lives, the nurses looking after him smeared blood on the face of his sleeping mother and accused her of eating him.*

When Pwyll heard the charge, he condemned his wife to sit outside his castle and greet every visitor with the story of her supposed crime. To complete her humiliation, she was then obliged to carry the visitor into the castle on her back like a horse.

Meanwhile, across the country, a man called Teyrnon was having trouble with his mare. It foaled annually on the night of the first of May; but come morning the foals were always gone. One year Teyrnon decided to solve the mystery by waiting overnight in the stable. No sooner had the mare given birth than a gigantic, clawed arm reached through the window to grab the new-born foal. Teyrnon drew his sword and severed the arm at the elbow. There was a howl from outside, but when he went to investigate, he could see nothing. On his return, however, he found a baby boy wrapped in silk.

He took the child home and reared him as his own. As the boy grew up, however, Teyrnon noticed that he looked just like Pwyll. Hearing the tale of Rhiannon, he put two and two together, and took the child to the castle. There he told Pwyll his story and presented the king with his son. Rhiannon was at once absolved of guilt, and at the ensuing feast she declared that her newly found son would henceforth be named Pryderi, or "Care", since his return had ended all the cares she had endured.

# Bran the Blessed

The story of Bendigeidfran, "Bran the Blessed", occupies the *Mabinogion*'s Second Branch. A giant of superhuman strength, Bran is associated with the ancient Celtic cult of the head – ultimately Bran is beheaded, but his head miraculously continues to speak. The head is finally buried under the "White Mount" in London, possibly the Tower, where it acts as a protective amulet for the island of Britain. Bran means "raven" and his story may lie at the root of the tradition that the kingdom will be safe as long as ravens are kept at the Tower.

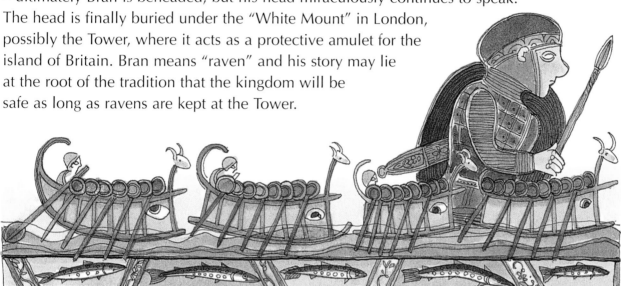

Bran's story opens with the marriage of his sister Branwen to Matholwch, king of Ireland. Tents were erected on the island of Anglesey – no house had yet been built that could contain Bran's huge bulk – and the wedding feast began. But amid the merriment one man was discontented. Piqued that nobody had asked his opinion on the marriage, Bran's half-brother Efnissyen went to the stables where Matholwch's horses were kept and sliced off their lips, tails, ears and eyelids.

Bewildered by this cruel and sudden discourtesy, Matholwch ordered his men back to their ships. Bran hurried to save the situation. He promised that Matholwch would have a new horse for every one that had been mutilated, plus a silver staff of his own height and a gold plate the size of his face. Still Matholwch hesitated. So Bran offered him the greatest treasure Wales possessed: a magic cauldron that could restore the dead to full health, except for their power of speech.

Mollified at last, Matholwch accepted the gifts and took his bride back to Ireland where, before the

**Bran the Blessed was said to be too big for any house or ship to hold. When he invaded Ireland he had to wade through the sea alongside his fleet (see page 84).**

year was out, she gave birth to a son, Gwern. But resentment at Efnissyen's insult lingered on, coming to a head in the year after Gwern's birth. It was decided that Branwen should be banished to a life of drudgery in the royal kitchen. To prevent Bran from hearing about this, Matholwch banned all ships from sailing to Britain and imprisoned incoming British crews. Branwen, however, reared a young starling and sent it to her brother with a message tied to its leg. Bran promptly mounted an invasion, leaving in charge six chiefs under the command of his son Caradawc (whose name is probably derived from that of Caratacus, a British leader who fought the Roman invaders in the first century AD). Shortly afterwards, Matholwch had news of an extraordinary apparition. A forest had

83

**A hand holding a severed head, from a Gaulish sanctuary, c.200BC. The Celtic belief that the soul resided in the head is reflected in the story of Bran (see opposite) and other myths.**

warrior. At a signal, the warriors would emerge and slaughter the Irish king's guests during a great feast. Bran was, indeed, impressed with the house, but Efnissyen was suspicious of the sacks. On being told that they contained only flour, he inspected one closely and felt the shape of a man's head. He squeezed the head between his thumb and forefinger until they met in the middle. He did the same to all one hundred sacks before finally declaring himself satisfied.

Somewhat disgruntled, Matholwch abandoned his plot, but the banquet went ahead as planned. During the feast, in which Matholwch agreed to abdicate in favour of Gwern, Efnissyen asked if he might be permitted to caress the child. Permission was granted, and Gwern approached across the hall – whereupon Efnissyen seized him and hurled him onto the fire.

The banquet at once became a bloody brawl in which the Irish soon got the upper hand, because they possessed the cauldron that brought all their dead warriors back to life. Efnissyen, however, hid himself under a pile of Irish corpses and was thrown along with them into the cauldron, whereupon he stretched out and broke the vessel into four pieces. But the effort was too much for him: his heart burst and he destroyed himself as well.

After three days of bloodshed Bran's army was victorious, but at terrible cost. His force had been reduced to just seven men – among them his brother Manawyddan and Pwyll's son Pryderi – while Bran himself was dying from a poisoned arrow in the foot. On the Irish side, there remained only five pregnant women to repopulate the island. Branwen, realizing that two kingdoms had been destroyed on her account, died of grief.

Back in Britain, the regency had been overthrown by a rival of Bran's called Caswallawn (whose name, like that of Caradawc, seems to come from that of an ancient British ruler, in this case Cassivellaunus, who fought Julius Caesar during his abortive invasion of 54BC). Caswallawn proceeded to slay Caradawc's six chieftains with the help of a magic spell. Helpless to save his men, Caradawc too succumbed to grief and died.

materialized in the sea. And beside the forest was a mountain from which jutted a ridge flanked by two lakes. Unable to explain this phenomenon, Matholwch sought Branwen's advice. The forest, she said, was the British fleet coming to save her. What they thought was a mountain was in fact Bran himself, wading through the sea because no ship was big enough to carry him. The "ridge" was his nose, and the "lakes" were his eyes.

Matholwch was alarmed and hatched a plan. He would seek to pacify Bran by building the first house that was big enough to hold him, and not only him but his whole army as well. But Matholwch also plotted treachery: from every pillar of the house he would hang a sack containing an Irish

### The Wondrous Head

The dying Bran instructed the seven survivors of the Irish débâcle to cut off his head and carry it to London. On the way they would stop at Harlech and at Gwales, a Welsh Otherworld off the coast of Penvro (Pembrokeshire). Gwales had three doors, one of which would be closed. They would stay there eighty years in bliss, during which time the head would talk to them and sustain them. But if at the end of this time they opened the closed door, they would remember all their griefs. At that point they must hurry to London and bury the head under the "White Mount" (probably the Tower of London, built of white stone), where it would guard Britain forever against invaders. In Gwales they did as instructed and the magical head kept them in good spirits. But after eighty years, one of them opened the third door and at once all were filled with misery. They set out for London and buried the head under the White Mount, where it was said it stayed until Arthur dug it up. According to Arthur, the country would be defended by force alone.

# The Enchantment of Dyfed

When Pwyll died, his son Pryderi inherited the kingdom of Dyfed. He took a wife, Cigfa, and married Rhiannon to the magician Manawyddan. One day an impenetrable fog descended on the kingdom, and when it cleared the entire population of Dyfed had disappeared except for Pryderi, Cigfa, Manawyddan and Rhiannon. Thus begins the Third Branch of the *Mabinogion*. Manawyddan is related by name to the Irish sea god Manannan, but here he has lost all connections with the sea.

Pryderi, Cigfa, Rhiannon and Manawyddan at first tried to survive by hunting. On one outing, a white boar led the hounds of Pryderi and Manawyddan into a castle they had never seen before. Inside, Pryderi found a golden bowl next to a fountain. He touched the bowl and was instantly transfixed to the spot, unable to move or speak. The next day Rhiannon went to rescue him, but she too suffered the same fate. A thick mist then descended, and by the time it cleared the castle had vanished.

Manawyddan and Cigfa now had to fend for themselves. Unable to hunt without dogs, they turned their hands to farming. Each time their crop ripened, however, it disappeared overnight before Manawyddan could harvest it. One night he kept guard, and saw an army of mice carrying off the corn. He gave chase, but caught only one of the creatures, which was lagging behind the others. He returned home, swearing to hang the rodent. While

This golden bowl, decorated with circular Celtic sun symbols, is dated to *c.*800–400BC. When Pryderi and Rhiannon entered the strange castle, they were rooted to the spot by touching a magic golden bowl that they saw there. Such episodes resemble legends in the Arthurian saga in which a knight enters a mysterious castle and sees the Holy Grail.

**An army of mice – as it turns out, they are transformed humans – devastate the crops of Manawyddan.**

he was preparing a mouse-sized gallows, three men – a scholar, a priest and a bishop – came in turn to plead for its life. Eventually the bishop asked him to name his own price for freeing it. Manawyddan demanded first the return of Pryderi and Rhiannon, then the lifting of the spell on Dyfed, and finally that the bishop should explain who he was and why Dyfed had been enchanted in the first place.

It turned out that the bishop was a certain Llwyd, who had come to avenge the indignities suffered by Gwawl when Pwyll had tricked him out of marrying Rhiannon. The mice were the lords and ladies of his court, and the one Manawyddan had caught was Llwyd's own pregnant wife, slowed by her condition. Manawyddan thereupon handed over the mouse, Llwyd freed Pryderi and Rhiannon, and Dyfed was restored.

# The Virgin's Lap

The Fourth Branch of the *Mabinogion* centres on the divine dynasty of Don, which ruled the northern Welsh kingdom of Gwynedd. Don was a goddess, the Welsh equivalent of Ireland's Danu, and Don's children, like the Tuatha De Danann, were associated with skills and craftsmanship. The tales, however, are concerned not so much with Don as with her brother, Math, and his relationships with his various nephews and nieces.

Math, the king of Gwynedd, was a magician with supernatural connections. He was a powerful man, save for one weakness: he could only remain alive if his feet lay in the lap of a virgin at all times except when he led his armies in battle. The origin of this peculiar arrangement is obscure, but it may have represented a Celtic form of the Christian Creation story – as in the Garden of Eden, peace and prosperity depend on unsullied innocence – with the very Celtic touch that warfare has a life-sustaining energy of its own. In practical terms, however, it meant that Math stayed at home, leaving his nephews Gwydion and Gilfaethwy to travel the kingdom on government business.

The brothers made capable ministers, especially Gwydion, who was an accomplished warrior and bard and also, like his uncle, possessed magical powers. Fatefully, however, Gilfaethwy fell in love with Goewin, the virgin who was Math's current foot-holder. Unable to consummate his love while Math was in residence, he confided his problem to Gwydion, who hatched a plan to separate Goewin from the royal feet. Learning that Pryderi, the king of Dyfed, owned a herd of magnificent swine – the first such creatures ever seen in Britain – which had been sent him by Arawn, the king of the Otherworld of Annwn, Gwydion approached Math and suggested that he and Gilfaethwy ask

Pryderi to part with the pigs as a gift to Gwynedd. Math agreed, and so the two brothers set out for Pryderi's court with an escort of ten men.

Disguised as bards, they were welcomed into Pryderi's palace and before long Gwydion had enchanted everybody with his songs. He then begged Pryderi for the gift of his pigs. Reluctantly, Pryderi told him that they had come from Annwn on condition that he neither give them away nor sell them until they had bred double their number. But Gwydion had a solution. That night he used his magic to create twelve horses and twelve greyhounds, equipped with gold saddles and gold collars, which he presented to Pryderi the following day. Gwydion pointed out that although Pryderi could not sell or give the pigs there was nothing to stop him exchanging them. Pryderi agreed, and

Gwydion and his men left with the swine. They rode fast, for Gwydion had not told Pryderi that after a day the magic would wear off and the horses and dogs would disappear.

By the time they reached Gwynedd and had built a sty for the pigs, Pryderi had already mounted an army to regain his property, and Math had left his virgin to take command of the defensive action. Gilfaethwy seized his chance, and raped Goewin in Math's own bed.

Until Goewin's violation, the two Welsh kingdoms had existed in amity. Now they were at war. Until then, Gwynedd had been prosperous. Now the state and its king were both imperilled. But if the rape harmed Math, it did even greater damage to the immediate prospects of Gwydion and Gilfaethwy. When Math returned victorious from

# The Death of Pryderi

**The war between Gwynedd and Dyfed, caused by the machinations of the magician Gwydion, was to prove the undoing of Pryderi of Dyfed.**

The opposing forces met in battle in Arfon, a district of Gwynedd, and the armies of Dyfed were forced to retreat with heavy losses. They were pursued to a place called Nant Call, where there was great bloodshed on both sides. Finally, Pryderi called for a truce, and offered twenty-four hostages to Gwynedd as surety for his good intentions. However, sporadic fighting between the two armies continued, and Pryderi put

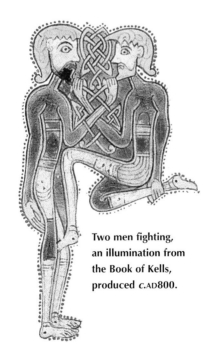

**Two men fighting, an illumination from the Book of Kells, produced c.AD800.**

forward another solution. He would meet Gwydion in single combat, since Gwydion alone had been responsible for the war. Math, the king of Gwynedd, agreed, and put the challenge to Gwydion, who announced: "I will pit my body against his gladly."
It might be expected that a climactic duel between two such important characters would be described in some detail, but the *Mabinogion* is surprisingly brief: "Those men were set apart and the equipping of them begun, and they fought. And by dint of strength and valour and by magic and enchantment Gwydion conquered, and Pryderi was slain."

the war, he compensated Goewin for the violation by making her his wife. Then he sought retribution on the brothers. He turned Gilfaethwy into a hind and Gwydion into a deer, and banished them to the forest with instructions to return in a year's time.

When the year was up the two arrived at Math's court, having mated and bred a fawn. Again Math touched them with his wand, turning the hind into a wild boar and the stag into a sow, and gave them the same instructions as before. But he kept the fawn, turning it into a human boy whom he named Hyddwn. The following year the two wild pigs arrived with a piglet. Math transformed the boar into a she-wolf, and the sow into a wolf, once again retaining their child, another boy, who was called Hychdwn. At the end of the third year the wolves came to Math with a cub which, as before, became a boy – Bleiddwn. Then, deciding that his nephews had endured enough humiliation, Math finally restored them to human form.

A Celtic stone head from the isle of Anglesey, perhaps from a druid shrine. It is traditionally said to represent the divine hero Lleu.

### Arianrhod and Lleu

Gwydion and Gilfaethwy had been pardoned. But there still remained a problem for the house of Gwynedd: finding a new virgin to hold Math's feet. Gwydion recommended his sister Arianrhod. Math put her to the test, by asking her to step over his magic wand. She did so, but in the process she gave birth to a boy with yellow hair. Math pounced, and took the baby. As Arianrhod fled the room she gave birth to another boy. Only Gwydion noticed this and quickly scooped the baby up in a silk cloth.

The yellow-haired baby was a precocious child. Shortly after his birth he ran to the sea and plunged in, finding himself as much at home in the waves as on dry land. For this ability he was named Dylan Eil Ton, "Sea, Son of the Wave".

Dylan's twin had a more troubled upbringing. For a while Gwydion kept him in a chest at the foot of his bed, then later fostered him out to a local woman. The boy grew at an enormous pace, and by the age of two was grown-up enough to go to court, where he lived under Gwydion's care. At the age of four he was taken by Gwydion to meet Arianrhod. But instead of being pleased to see her son, Arianrhod was angry at being reminded of her shame. She asked what his name was, at which Gwydion suddenly remembered that he had no name. So Arianrhod cursed the boy never to have a name unless it was bestowed by herself.

The next day, Gwydion made a magic ship out of seaweed and the two of them sailed to Arianrhod's castle disguised as cobblers. When Arianrhod came aboard to be fitted for a pair of shoes, the boy flung a stone and killed a wren that had just alighted on the deck. "The fair boy has a deft hand," she remarked, at which Gwydion turned the ship back into seaweed and stood, his disguise gone, with the boy. "He now has a name, thanks to you: Lleu Llaw Gyffes, 'Bright One of the Deft Hand'". Furious at being tricked, Arianrhod put another curse on Lleu: he would never bear arms unless she gave them to him herself.

So Gwydion took Lleu away and trained him to become a warrior, before taking him back to Arianrhod's castle. This time they were disguised as bards. They spent the evening entertaining, then

# The Enigma of Lleu

*Lleu was associated with supernatural beings and he was probably a god in origin. His name ("Bright One") is related to that of Ireland's god Lugh and the Celtic god Lugus. His life is stamped with elements of divinity and magic. For example, he can only attain a name, weapons and a wife – in other words, the attributes of manhood – through magical intervention.*

Lleu's wife Blodeuwedd, in particular, signals his affinity with nature rather than humanity. On top of this, his existence is riddled with paradox. He was born to a virgin and could only die in near-impossible circumstances. The weapon that killed him had to be a spear made when work was normally forbidden, on Sundays when everybody else was at Mass. Forging the spear was the easy part, because Lleu could not die in a house or in the open, on land or on water, on foot or on horseback, clothed or naked. In fact, as he revealed to Blodeuwedd, the only way in which he could be killed was if a bathtub was built for him under a thatched roof. If a billy goat then stood beside the tub and Lleu, half-dressed, stood with one foot on its back and the other foot on the side of the tub – only then could he be killed, if struck by the spear. Like Samson telling Delilah the source of his strength in the biblical story, Lleu revealed these conditions to the treacherous Blodeuwedd. Yet even when the unlikely circumstances were fulfilled there remained an enigma: when Blodeuwedd's lover Gronw struck Lleu with the spear, he did not die, but mutated into a bird.

the following morning Gwydion went to work with his magic, creating the illusion of a massive invasion fleet. Arianrhod hastily equipped the couple with armour and weapons for the forthcoming battle, at which point Gwydion revealed the deception. Incensed, Arianrhod therefore made a final curse: that Lleu would never have a human wife. Gwydion went to Math and sought his uncle's help in confounding this latest curse. Together they conjured up a magical woman out of the flowers of the oak, the broom and the meadowsweet, and presented her to Lleu. At the same time Math granted Lleu some territory of his own, in which he set up court with his new bride, whose name was Blodeuwedd, literally "Flower-Face".

Blodeuwedd, however, was unfaithful. She took a lover, a neighbouring chieftain called

**Blodeuwedd, the woman of flowers.**

Gronw, and plotted with him to kill Lleu. It was no easy task, because Lleu's death was surrounded by a host of magical preconditions. But eventually Gronw succeeded in stabbing Lleu with a spear, and abandoned him to die.

Gwydion's revenge was swift. He set off after the lovers. Gronw was despatched with a spear, in the same place and manner that he had tried to kill Lleu (see next page). As for Blodeuwedd, when she heard Gwydion was coming she fled with her maids into the hills. But they were so busy looking back that they fell into a lake and all were drowned except for Blodeuwedd herself. Gwydion transformed her into an owl, doomed, according to folklore, to be hated by all other birds and for that reason only able to come out at night. This story served to explain the origin of the older Welsh word for "owl": *blodeuwedd*.

# The Triumph of Lleu

*When Lleu was speared by Gronw he did not die. Instead, to his opponent's surprise, he turned into an eagle and flew away. As soon as Gwydion heard of this, he made it a priority to find Lleu. He journeyed all over Wales without finding any trace of his nephew, and was on the point of despair when he stopped for a night at a peasant's house in Arfon, a district of Gwynedd.*

*Below: An eagle, from the Book of Durrow, an Irish illuminated manuscript of c.AD650.*

During his stay with the peasant, Gwydion heard of a peculiar sow which his host owned. Every morning, as soon as the sty was opened, the sow would rush out and disappear into the countryside, returning only late at night. There was nothing the peasant could do to stop it, and he had not the faintest idea where it went.

Intrigued, Gwydion waited by the sty the following morning. As soon as the door was opened, he set off after the sow. He followed it upstream to a valley, where it started to gorge itself on something that lay beneath a tree. Coming closer, Gwydion saw that the pig was eating maggots and lumps of decayed flesh. And looking up to the top of the tree, he saw an eagle. Every time it shook itself, a shower of rotten flesh fell to the ground.

Convinced that the eagle was Lleu, Gwydion sang it a song. Hearing it, the eagle came down to the middle of the tree. Gwydion sang another song and the eagle came down to the lowest branch. When Gwydion sang a third song the eagle dropped down onto his knee. Gwydion touched the scrawny bird with his wand and, sure enough, it changed back into Lleu. But because of his wound he was in pitiful shape, nothing but skin and bone, and it took a full year and the attentions of the best doctors in Gwynedd

before he was completely restored to health. When Gronw heard of Lleu's return, he hastily sent him a placatory message, offering compensation for the wrong done to him. Would he prefer land or money? Lleu replied that he wanted neither. The only compensation he would accept was if Gronw stood by the river as he himself had done, and allowed Lleu to throw a spear at him. Reluctantly – and only after having petitioned his brothers, nobles and soldiers to take his place – Gronw agreed. Yet he had one small hope of survival. Would it be permissible, he asked, since after all he had only been acting under the influence of an evil woman, to hold a stone in front of him as Lleu threw the spear? Lleu agreed. But the stone did Gronw no good – Lleu's spear passed right through the solid rock and hit Gronw squarely in the chest, killing him instantly. Lleu regained his lands and in due course, after the death of Math, became ruler of all Gwynedd. And for ever afterwards, on the bank of the river Cynfael, the stone stood with the spear sticking through it as a reminder of his triumph over Gronw. The spot was called Llech Ronw ("Stone of Gronw").

# Culhwch, the Royal Hero

Culhwch is the first great hero of Welsh mythology. Although his adventures, recounted in the story *Culhwch and Olwen*, follow the Four Branches that make up the main body of the *Mabinogion*, they contain traces of Old Welsh that suggest the story may originally have taken shape centuries earlier. In fact, with its magic, shape-shifting, giants, monsters, fabulous animals and great lists of unlikely deeds and characters, the tale of Culhwch is rooted firmly in the most ancient traditions of Celtic myth.

Like many Celtic heroes, Culhwch came into the world in bizarre circumstances. Queen Goleudd-ydd, his mother, went mad during her pregnancy, and eventually gave birth to a son amidst a herd of pigs. The swineherd reared the child and brought him to the court, where he was given the name of Culhwch, or "Pig Run". Shortly after, Goleuddydd fell mortally ill, and made her husband promise never to remarry until a thorn grew on her grave. Every morning, for seven years, the king visited her grave to check its condition, unaware that Goleudd-ydd had ordered her servant to keep it well-mown. One year, however, the servant forgot to mow the grave, a thorn grew, and the king took a new wife.

The king's new bride – whom he obtained by killing her husband – brought with her a daughter, and on meeting Culhwch she tried to set up a match. Culhwch refused, on the grounds that he was too young, whereupon his stepmother made a prophecy: that he would never sleep with a woman until he had won the hand of Olwen, daughter of Ysbaddaden, the chief of the giants. Culhwch fell in love with Olwen just at the mention of her name. When he reported this to his father, the king dismissed it airily. "Go to Arthur," he said. "He is your first cousin. Have him trim your hair then ask him to obtain Olwen for you."

Although he bears the name of the great monarch of medieval legend, the Arthur Culhwch was sent to meet is a very Celtic figure, more of a warrior chief than a paragon of courtly chivalry. Yet his court was apparently already a splendid place, for the young hero prepared for his visit with a display of finery worthy of Camelot itself. Culhwch finally set off in magnificent style, on a white horse with a greyhound running on either side, wearing a pair of golden thigh boots and a purple cloak which had golden apples embroidered on each corner. He

**Culhwch rides to Arthur's court. His two hounds have Otherworldly associations.**

carried two silver spears, a gold sword, an ivory-embossed shield "the colour of lightning" and a battle axe "which would draw blood from the wind". Thus, with the hounds weaving intricate patterns around horse and rider as they walked, and the horse's hooves throwing up dainty clods of earth "as if they were four swallows in the air overhead", he arrived at Arthur's castle. Hounds and apples are associated with magic and the Otherworld, suggesting that the human Culhwch may originally have been a divine figure.

For all Culhwch's splendour, the gatekeeper refused to let him in. Arthur was feasting, Culhwch was told, and nobody could enter except a king or a craftsman. Culhwch threatened dire consequences. If not let in he would give three shouts which would be heard in Cornwall, Scotland and Ireland, and any pregnant woman who heard them would miscarry, while every other woman would become barren. The gatekeeper opened the door.

Without bothering to dismount Culhwch rode up to the table, where Arthur graciously granted him honorary royal status and invited him to join his guests. But instead of sitting down, Culhwch demanded a favour: that Arthur cut his hair. The favour was granted, and when Culhwch revealed his identity Arthur was even more fulsome in his hospitality. He granted him any other favour he wanted, and Culhwch asked for the hand of Olwen, the daughter of Chief Giant Ysbaddaden (presumably, although it is never actually stated, Olwen herself was of normal human size). Culhwch invoked her in the name of each member of Arthur's court. This roll-call of some two hundred and sixty notable men, women, horses, dogs and swords must have been something of a *tour-de-force* for the bards who recited the tale from memory. Starting with famous heroes such as Cei and Bedwyr (the originals of the knights Kay and Bedivere in Arthurian romances) and Fercus Ap Roch (the

Fergus mac Roich of Irish myth), the list moves on to such characters as Ceudawg Half-Wit, Sol Osol, whose heroic ability was that of standing on one foot all day, Ellylw daughter of Neol Hang Cock, Suck son of Sucker, Enough son of Surfeit and Conyn and his eighteen brothers, the sons of Caw. The sons of giants, the sons of dwarves, men with enormous beards, men with huge lips, the steward of Devon and Cornwall, the best leaper of Ireland, one bishop and at least three kings of France – all, great and small and in-between, featured in Culhwch's list, as well as the leading maidens of the land in their golden torques.

Culhwch had invoked his two hundred and sixtieth name before Arthur finally intervened. "I have not heard anything of this girl," he said, "nor of her parents, but I will gladly send messengers to learn of her." And so, Arthur and his warriors embarked upon the quest for Olwen, the daughter of Chief Giant Ysbaddaden.

## The Quest for Olwen

The use of a great quest as a framework for a mythic narrative is probably an ancient bardic device. There are other aspects of Culhwch's quest which betray its ancient origins, notably the appearance of a figure called Mabon son of Modron, who is almost certainly an ancient British and Gaulish god associated with hunting.

Arthur's messengers scoured the land for a year in the search for Olwen, but to no avail. At this, Culhwch lost his patience and threatened to ruin Arthur's reputation as a man who kept his word. But Cei intervened with the suggestion that he and Culhwch seek Olwen together. With them they took Bedwyr and Cynddilig, Arthur's tracker, as well as the interpreter Gwrhyr, who could speak all languages, and Menw, who could cast spells of invisibility. After they had travelled for some distance they spied a castle

The name of Conyn or "Stalk", a hero invoked by Culhwch before Arthur, recalls Celtic rulers whose emblem was a stalk of wheat, as on this coin of the British king Cunobelinus (ruled AD10–40).

on the horizon. It was so large that they had to travel for several more days before it appeared to be even slightly nearer. As they approached they saw a shepherd tending a scattered flock with the aid of a mastiff the size of a small horse. When he learned of their quest, the shepherd warned them never to mention it to Chief Giant Ysbaddaden, because no one who had asked for his daughter's hand had ever lived to tell the tale. He himself, the shepherd explained, was Custennin, Ysbaddaden's brother, and had good cause to fear him: the giant had killed all but one of his sons. Custennin then took the company home to meet his wife.

The shepherd's wife, it transpired, was Culhwch's aunt. She was delighted to see her nephew and agreed to assist him. Olwen, she revealed, came to their house every Saturday to wash her hair and was due to come the following day. In due course

Olwen arrived dressed in a robe of flame-coloured silk and adorned with golden jewellery studded with emeralds and rubies. As she walked, white flowers sprang up in her wake.

When Olwen met Culhwch she fell in love with him and told him to ask her father for her hand because she had sworn never to marry without his permission. She warned that Ysbaddaden would do everything he could to put Culhwch off, because it was his destiny to die on the day she married.

The next day they visited Ysbaddaden in his castle. He made various excuses for not seeing them that day and, as they turned to leave, he threw a poisoned spear at them. Bedwyr caught it and flung it back, piercing Ysbaddaden through the kneecap and eliciting a torrent of elaborate abuse. The next day they went to Ysbaddaden and were again given excuses. As they left Ysbaddaden threw a second

# Mabon, son of Modron

*Mabon, the son of Modron – their names mean "Son" and "Mother" – is a puzzling character. His kidnapping, at three days old, is similar to Pryderi's, and he may be a version of the same figure.*

**A stone head (c.100–400AD) of Maponus, found at Corbridge in Northumberland. The hollow on the top was probably for drink-offerings.**

But other intriguing elements form part of Mabon's background. His father is never named, so he is simply "the Son of the Mother". Modron herself was a pre-Christian mother goddess, and her name is identical in origin to that of a mother goddess worshipped in Gaul by the name of Matrona, "The Divine Mother", who gave her name to the river Marne. Mabon's name is probably identical to that of Maponus, a youth deity who had a cult following in the Roman period in both Britain and Gaul. His worship was linked with that of the Roman Apollo, since both gods were associated with hunting, poetry and music. Maponus the hunter can still be clearly discerned in the figure of Mabon, whose presence is essential to Arthur's hunt for the boar Twrch Trwyth. As a "divine youth" Mabon can be equated with Oenghus, the god of love in Irish mythology, who is alternatively known as Mac Og or "Young Son".

poisoned spear which Menw caught and threw back so that it pierced the giant's chest. Ysbad aden's language grew even more colourful. On t third day the same thing happened, but this tir Culhwch caught the spear and sent it flying back. pierced Ysbaddaden's eye and brought forth mo howls of invective from the injured giant.

On the fourth day Ysbaddaden finally gave i Culhwch could marry Olwen, he said, but or once Culhwch had fulfilled a number of tasks f him. Ysbaddaden then reeled off a list of for impossible-sounding requests. They included wir ning a magic horn and cauldron and a giant's sword, as well as finding honey nine times sweeter than a bee's for the wedding feast.

The most onerous task, however, was to acquire a set of shears, razor and comb witl which the giant would groom himself for Olwer wedding. But this equipment lay between the ea of a ferocious giant boar, Twrch Trwyth, who ha once been a king but had been transformed intc monstrous animal because of his evil ways.

To each of the giant's requests Culhwch gave a firm reply: "That is simple, although you do not think it is. I shall accomplish that task and marry your daughter – and you will die."

One of the tasks set by Ysbaddaden was to obtain the "cauldron of Diwrnach". This head is from a 1st-century BC bronze cauldron discovered at Rynkeby in Denmark.

## Mabon and the End of the Quest

One of the many tasks which Culhwch had to perform before going after Twrch Trywth was to obtain the services of a certain Mabon son of Modron as huntsman. Mabon had not been seen or heard of since he had been stolen from his mother when he was only three days old. Gwrhyr the interpreter (see page 92) enquired first of the Ouzel of Cilgwri, one of the oldest creatures in existence. The Ouzel had never heard of Mabon, but sent Gwrhyr to an even older creature, the Stag of Redynvre. The Stag knew nothing, but led them to the Owl of Cwm Cawlwyd who was older still. The Owl in turn directed them to the Eagle of Gwernabwy, a creature yet more ancient. When he had first come to the world he had possessed a stone from the top of which he could peck the stars. But now he was so old that the

stone had worn down until it was no higher than a hand's breadth. The Eagle, however, knew nothing and sent them to the Salmon of Llyn Llyw, the oldest of all living things. This recalls Irish stories of omniscient long-lived beings who took the form of a salmon, such as Fintan (see page 48). The Salmon directed them to Gloucester and there Arthur's men found Mabon locked in a dungeon. They carried him off to safety before continuing on their next mission.

The preparations for the boar hunt did not stop with the freeing of Mabon. There were many other tasks, of an equally arduous nature, to fulfill. Ysbaddaden had insisted, for example, that the boar be hunted with a certain dog, Drudwyn, who belonged to a certain Greid son of Eri. Obtaining the hound was hard enough, but first of all they had

# The Hunting of Twrch Trwyth

*In their hunt for Twrch Trwyth, Arthur's men had to contend not only with the boar but also its seven fierce piglets. They ran their quarry down to Ireland, where the battle to win the scissors, comb and razor from the boar started in earnest.*

By the time Arthur caught up with the brood, they had devastated much of Ireland and moved on to Wales. Day after day the pursuit continued, and many warriors died in its course. At last, all the piglets were killed, but by that time Twrch Trwyth was heading for Cornwall. There

he was driven into a river, where Mabon snatched the razor and scissors. But the boar regained his footing and rampaged further before the comb could also be retrieved. When that feat was eventually accomplished, the beast fled into the sea, and was never heard of again.

to accomplish an even harder task – finding a leash to control it. The leash, they learnt, could only be made from hair taken from the beard of Dillius, a giant warrior. To make matters more difficult, they could not simply kill him and shave the beard because then the hairs would be too brittle and weak. Instead they had to pluck them from his chin while he was still alive, using a pair of wooden tweezers. They waited until Dillius had fallen asleep after a heavy meal, then Cei knocked him senseless. The company plucked Dillius's chin bald before finally killing him.

One by one, the various preconditions to the hunt were fulfilled and at length the company set out after Twrch Trwyth. The chase was a long and bloody one, ranging throughout Ireland, Wales and Cornwall (see above). Many of Arthur's most

famous warriors perished in the attempt, but at long last the razor, scissors and comb were snatched from between the boar's ears.

"Is there any of the marvels still unobtained?" asked Arthur. "Yes," replied one of his men. "The blood of the Black Witch, daughter of the White Witch, from the head of the Valley of Grief in the uplands of Hell." So off they went, and found the hag in her cave. Two brothers were sent in after her, but they were both disarmed, beaten and driven out "squealing and squalling". Arthur sent another two of his men into the cave, but they suffered a similar fate. By the time the witch had finished with them, all four men had to be loaded like sacks onto the back of Arthur's horse.

Outraged at the indignity suffered by his men, Arthur himself went forward. Standing at the cave entrance he took aim with his knife and threw it at the witch, slicing her neatly through the middle "until she was as two tubs". One of Arthur's men, a certain Cadw of Prydein, collected the witch's blood and then Arthur and his followers, their last task completed, headed for Ysbaddaden's castle.

When they arrived, Cadw of Prydein was given the task of shaving the giant, while Culhwch watched gloatingly. When the last hair had been shaved off, Culhwch demanded Olwen's hand. Ysbaddaden granted it, with ill grace. "Do not bother thanking me," he said. "You should thank Arthur. It was he who got her for you. If it had been up to me you would never have had her." Ysbaddaden then declared that the time had come for him to die. At this, the giant's nephew Goreu, the son of Custennin, dragged Ysbaddaden away and killed him behind the castle. Goreu stuck his uncle's head on a stake and took possession of the castle and all his lands. Ysbaddaden was no more.

Culhwch and Olwen were married that very night, and they both lived happily together for the rest of their lives. Arthur's men dispersed to their own homes. The quest was over.

# Shorter Tales

Apart from the Four Branches and the heroic saga of Culhwch, the *Mabinogion* includes three shorter tales containing clear traces of ancient mythology: *The Dream of Macsen*, *Lludd and Llefelys* and *The Dream of Rhonabwy*. These tales stand on the cusp between Celtic myth and the the medieval Arthurian cycle. Arthur features in the last of these, but as in *Culhwch and Olwen*, he is still more of a Celtic chieftain than a chivalrous king.

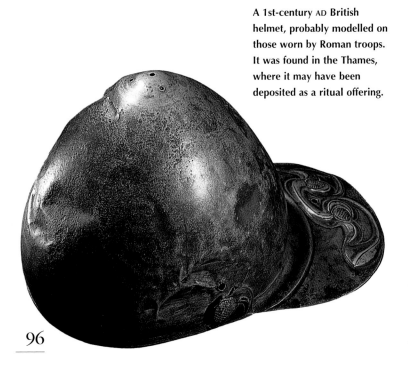

**A 1st-century AD British helmet, probably modelled on those worn by Roman troops. It was found in the Thames, where it may have been deposited as a ritual offering.**

*The Dream of Macsen* is based on the true story of Magnus Maximus, a fourth-century AD Roman general stationed in Britain who made a failed bid to become Roman emperor. Maximus, who was born in Spain, made his name by successfully defending Roman Britain against the Picts and Scots. In the spring of AD383 his British troops declared him emperor and he launched an invasion of the Roman Empire, which at that time was administered in two parts: the Western Empire, ruled jointly by the emperors Gratian and Valentinian II, and the Eastern Empire, ruled by Theodosius I.

Historically, Maximus defeated and killed Gratian and became master of Gaul and Spain. Rather than see the empire torn apart by civil war, Valentinian and Theodosius recognized Maximus as ruler of the captured lands. But Maximus wanted more, and in AD387 he overran Italy and forced Valentinian to flee to Theodosius in Constantinople.

# The Dream of Macsen

*In the story of this name included in the* **Mabinogion**, **Macsen**, *unlike the historical* **Magnus Maximus**, *is depicted as the true emperor of Rome. He has to recapture his throne from a usurper, a feat he accomplishes only with the help of British warriors. The story starts in Rome, where Macsen dreams that he has met the most beautiful woman in the world.*

*Below left*: **A portrait of the emperor Magnus Maximus on one of the gold coins issued during his brief reign.**
*Bottom*: **On a hunting expedition, Macsen lay down to rest in the shade of his men's shields. He fell asleep and dreamed of the beautiful Elen.**

When Macsen awoke, he set about tracking down the woman he had seen in his dream. Messengers were sent to retrace his dream voyage. From the peak of Snowdon, the highest mountain in Wales, they finally spotted the castle in which she lived.

When the lady, whose name turned out to be Elen, was informed of the reason for their coming, she proudly informed them that if the emperor was in love with her, then he should come to seek her for himself. Macsen duly arrived with an army, having conquered Britain en route.

Elen agreed to wed him, but asked as a wedding gift that her father should be made governor of Britain. She also requested that the three islands of Britain – Wight, Man and Anglesey – become her own personal property.

Macsen lived with his bride in Britain, which experienced a time of great prosperity and peace. After seven years, however, the Romans chose a new emperor in Macsen's place. The usurped ruler hurried back to Italy to reclaim the throne, but all his attempts to capture the city of Rome itself proved unsuccessful.

Then, a year after he had undertaken the siege, a band of British warriors arrived, commanded by Elen's two brothers. They assessed the situation and spotted a weak point: the rival emperors stopped fighting at noon each day so that their troops could rest. Timing their assault for the midday break, the Britons managed to storm the city.

Their reward from Macsen for this feat matched their achievement. Reinstalled on the throne, the emperor gave his British troops a free hand to pillage, and many years passed before they decided to return to their homeland.

Theodosius launched a counter-attack and in AD388 Maximus was defeated by Valentinian at Aquileia (near modern Venice) and beheaded.

Although their leader had been defeated, the Britons who had been the linchpin of Maximus's army must have returned home with heroic tales of what was certainly the greatest military adventure of their lives. The story of Macsen looks back with nostalgia (not to mention some exaggeration) to those heady days of imperial glory, when the might of Rome depended on British fighting men.

## Lludd and Llefelys

The story of Lludd and Llefelys is linked to the tale of Macsen by the divine figure of Lludd's father Beli, the ruler of Britain said to have been overthrown by Macsen. There is a historical connection too: one of Lludd's brothers is Caswallawn, a character derived from Cassivellaunus, a powerful British king who fought against Julius Caesar in 55–54BC. Lludd also plays a part in the tale of Culhwch and Olwen, while his alternative name, Nudd, links him to Nuadu, the king of the Tuatha De Danann in Irish myth (see page 52). In Geoffrey of Monmouth's *History of the Kings of Britain, c.*1136, Lludd appears as King Lud, a mythical British king. He entered English folklore as the founder of London, which

was said to be named after him, and according to tradition he is recalled in the city's Ludgate Hill. In the Welsh tale, Lludd inherited the kingdom of Britain from Beli and chose London as his residence. He strengthened its fortifications, and ordered the inhabitants to build magnificent homes.

When the king of France died, he left his kingdom to his unmarried daughter. Lludd hastened to put forward his brother Llefelys as a prospective husband for the young woman. Llefelys was accepted and left to rule France, but soon afterwards Britain suffered a series of plagues. The first took the form of a magical race of invaders, the Coranieid, whose ears were so keen that they could hear on the wind every conversation in the island. The second was a terrifying dragon's scream which could be heard throughout the land every May Day Eve. It caused women to miscarry, men to faint, children to go mad and animals to become barren. The third plague affected Lludd's court in particular.

**Two dragons fighting on May Day Eve. The scream of one of the dragons on the eve of May Day caused madness, infertility and confusion throughout the kingdom of Lludd.**

# The Mystic Centre

***In order to vanquish the two dragons, Lludd had first to find the middle of his kingdom. For the Celts, the mystic centre or "navel" of the land was a powerful concept.***

The centre of the land was the focal point of its sacred energy, the place where the soul of the country resided. In the story of Lludd, the two dragons represent the Britons and the Saxons, fighting for the heart and soul of the country. The British dragon raised a scream that rendered the land barren at the early summer festival of Beltane at the start of May, the very time that was supposed to herald the most fertile season of the year. To make the dragons harmless, they had to be taken far from the centre of the land to the mountains of north Wales.

Ireland was divided into five provinces, each of which represented one of the four directions, with the former province of Meath as the "centre". The centre of Meath itself was Tara, the capital of the High Kings of Ireland. It was here that the king was installed and ritually married to a goddess who personified Ireland. She resided in a stone called *Lia Fail* ("Stone of Destiny"), which stood at Tara. When a contender for the kingship presented himself at the stone, it was said to utter a cry if the goddess approved of the candidate.

Caesar claimed that the druids of Gaul assembled once a year at a sacred spot in the lands of the Carnutes, "whose territory is reckoned as the centre of all Gaul". Some tribal capitals in Gaul were named *Mediolanon* ("Middle of the Land"), which may reflect their spiritual as well as political significance.

No matter how much food was stored in the royal larders, it all disappeared almost at once. A year's supply of provisions would be gone within a day.

Perplexed, Lludd sought Llefelys's advice. He fitted out a fleet in complete silence and sailed towards France to meet his brother, at the head of his own fleet, halfway across the Channel. So that the Coranieid might not hear them, they spoke to each other through a long horn. But everything they said came out as the opposite of what they intended – a sign, said Llefelys, that the horn was possessed by a devil. They washed the devil out with wine and continued their secret conversation.

Llefelys whispered a cure for the first plague. He would give Lludd some insects which he must mash into a potion and then sprinkle over the invaders. The mixture would poison the Coranieid but would be harmless to his own people. The second plague, he muttered, was caused by a British dragon screaming as it fought a foreign one. The cure for this was to find the exact centre of the kingdom, trick the dragons into a pit and bury them in a stone chest for evermore. The third plague was more difficult to deal with. It resulted from a gigantic magician thieving Lludd's food when all were asleep. Lludd must wait up for him, Llefelys breathed, and if he felt sleepy he must stand in a vat of cold water to wake himself up.

Lludd agreed to everything and returned at once to his kingdom. He crushed the insects in water, then summoned everyone in the land, including the Coranieid, to his court under the pretence of making peace between the two races. When all were assembled he threw the potion over the assembly and, sure enough, his own people remained unscathed while the Coranieid perished.

For his next task Lludd had the whole of Britain measured from top to bottom and side to side, and discovered the exact centre to be the city of Oxford. He had a pit dug there and placed in it a vat of the best mead, covered with a silk cloth. The dragons came out fighting, stepped on the silk and at once sank into the mead where they were quickly overcome by the alcoholic fumes. Lludd wrapped the creatures up in the cloth, locked them in a stone chest, and had them taken to Dinas

Emrys in the mountains of north Wales, where they were buried. Other legends recount how the dragons were later found by the magician Merlin.

There now remained only the curse of the giant to be dealt with. A feast was laid out and Lludd stood guard. Gradually everyone else fell asleep, but Lludd stayed awake and saw a large man in armour enter the hall and stuff all the provisions into a seemingly bottomless basket. Lludd chased after him and challenged him. The two drew swords and fought until sparks flew. Eventually, however, Lludd brought his opponent to his knees, and the tale ends with him sparing the giant, who promised from then on to be a faithful servant.

## The Dream of Rhonabwy

The most literary and probably in origin the latest tale in the *Mabinogion* is *The Dream of Rhonabwy*, written *c*.AD1200, which looks forward to the medieval Arthurian romances while simultaneously casting wistful glances at the Celtic past. Arthur is portrayed here as he prepares to meet the Anglo-Saxons at the battle of Mount Badon, a probably historical but still unlocated engagement that took

A bronze raven from a cache of Roman-period ritual objects found in Norfolk. In Rhonabwy's dream, Owein's army was made up of ravens.

place *c*.AD520 and which, legend has it, claimed the lives of nearly a thousand Saxon chiefs. The action centres on the typically Celtic theme of infighting: Greek and Roman commentators observed that the Celts loved quarrelling, and if they had no foes to hand they would happily fight among themselves. Arthur and his follower, Owein, play *gwyddbwyll* (a board game similar to chess) while their two armies quarrel in the background. A surreal note is added by the fact that Owein's army consists of three hundred ravens, creatures associated with the ancient Celtic war goddesses. From one of these goddesses, the Irish Morrigan, Owein's mother Morgan Le Fay was derived (see page 119). Owein himself became the Yvain of Arthurian romance (see page 120).

Rhonabwy is described as a warrior in the service of King Madawg of Powys, a historical Welsh ruler who died in AD1159. Madawg's brother Iorweth – another historical figure – had been raiding England, and Rhonabwy was among those sent to stop him. While he was in Powys, he found himself billeted in a house of unspeakable squalor: the floor was uneven and covered in cow dung and urine. Smoke filled the room from a fire tended by an old hag, and the bed was flea-ridden and rough. Despairing of sleep, Rhonabwy lay down on the least uncomfortable place that he could find in the hovel – a yellow cowskin. Falling into a deep slumber, he found himself transported into a magnificent dreamworld.

Rhonabwy and his men were standing on a plain. As they stared around, a huge warrior rode up, dressed in green and yellow. He pulled them onto his saddle and took them to Arthur's court. Once there, they felt the full weight of their insignificance. Everything was grand – the people, their clothes, their deportment. Arthur scoffed at Rhonabwy's troop. "I am laughing," he said, "because it is sad to see such miserable specimens guarding the island compared with the men who held it before."

The troops at Arthur's command presented a very different spectacle. Some were dressed all in red, others all in black. One man wore white mail pierced with red rivets, another a costume of red brocade interwoven with yellow silk. Two armies – the soldiers of Norway and Denmark – arrived in harlequin dress. The Norwegians were wearing white cloaks fringed with black, while the Danes were clad in the same colour scheme in reverse.

As these and other colourfully dressed warriors mustered for battle, Arthur calmly sat down and arranged a set of gold *gwyddbwyll* pieces on a silver board. He then challenged one of his best warriors, Owein son of Urien, to a game. Arthur and Owein were deep in the game when one of Owein's pages reported that Arthur's men were harassing Owein's ravens. Owein remonstrated with Arthur, but the only response he got was: "Your move". Soon after, another page informed Owein that now his ravens were being stabbed. "Your move," said Arthur. Then a third page arrived with the news that the ravens were now being massacred. Arthur was unperturbed. "Play on," he said.

Owein then gave permission for his ravens to counter-attack. Now it was the turn of Arthur's pages to complain that the king's men were being threatened. "Play on," said Owein. Finally a page announced that so many of Arthur's retinue had been killed that he would be hard pressed to defend the island of Britain. At that point Arthur angrily demanded that Owein call off his birds, and Owein at last relented. The game was over. And so, temporarily, was the battle of Badon. Arthur and his foe agreed to a month's truce. As Cei, Arthur's foremost knight, was summoning the men to be ready in a month, Rhonabwy awoke in the hovel. He had been asleep for three days and nights.

"No bard or storyteller is able to recite the *Dream* by heart," says the *Mabinogion*. This is a telling remark, for in the years to come a new style of epic, imported from the Continent, would become prominent. Its style, while beautiful and elegant in its own right, would contain little of the traditional repetition, alliteration and rhythmic patterns that had enabled Celtic storytellers to recount the old sagas from memory. *The Dream of Rhonabwy*, therefore, is one of the last links with the great bardic tradition of the Celts. The irony is that this tradition was largely supplanted by a new foreign genre – the romance – whose chief inspiration was a figure drawn from old Celtic legend: King Arthur.

**Arthur and Owein play *gwyddbwyll*, in which a single king was pursued by the men of the other side.**

MAGNUS ARTURUS REX DOMINUS LUNCELOT DU LAC
POTENTISSIMUS ANGLIAE EQUES INVICTUS

# LEGENDS OF ARTHUR

Arthur is more than just a character from Celtic myth: he is an international phenomenon. When tales of his extraordinary deeds and heroic entourage first hit Europe in about the eleventh century they were an instant and spectacular success. Here was a figure who perfectly embodied the growing cult of chivalry, the ideal of the just and noble ruler, whose knights were fighters for justice and paragons of bravery. Arthur's popularity alarmed some churchmen, however, who were concerned that their flock might prefer the secular stories of the knights of the Round Table to the holy Word of God.

These vivid tales of love and war, adventure and adultery, piety and betrayal began life as scattered legends in early medieval British chronicles, romances attached to the Welsh *Mabinogion*, and Breton lays (short poems usually narrating a single episode). From these grew one of the most enduring stories ever known, kept alive in our own time by films, plays, operas and novels. Names such as Merlin, Excalibur, Camelot, Morgan Le Fay, Tristan, Lancelot and Avalon are still familiar today.

Arthur emerged in the medieval chronicles of Britain as a *dux bellorum*, or "war leader", rather than as an actual king. The chronicles portray him as a valiant warrior who, with his noble followers, fought to preserve the remnants of the crumbling Roman Empire. From this beginning his legend developed in two main directions: romances of courtly love and tales of the Holy Grail. Yet beneath the literary trappings lies a plain tale of action and passion that appealed to the medieval descendants of the Celts and their neighbours as they struggled in the face of famine, plague and war. Medieval authors drew on a variety of pagan sources, including Celtic figures such as Guinevere and Morgan Le Fay, to create a world where, for a time at least, peace and justice reigned.

Many of the narratives centre around the conflict between pagan values and Christian ideals. Even in the Grail stories, the focus is solidly upon humans as they repeatedly fail to live up to the spiritual perfection demanded by the medieval Church. The Arthurian legends are a celebration of what humans can create and a lamentation for what they destroy. They span the gap from Celtic times to the present, each new generation finding something fascinating and inspiring in these timeless tales.

**King Arthur and the knights of the Round Table, from a French manuscript of the 15th century. The Holy Grail stands in the centre of the table.**

*Opposite, above:* **Arthur and his most famous knight, Lancelot, in stained glass by William Morris (1834–96). The two originally appeared in separate story cycles.**

*Opposite, below:* **Arthur in battle, a 14th-century French illustration. The dragon banner probably refers to the king's family name, Pendragon.**

103

# The Historical Arthur

From the earliest mentions of Arthur, such as that in Nennius's *Historia Brittonum* ("The History of the Britons") of *c.*AD800, many people have believed that the legendary king and warrior really existed. In the late nineteenth century, the search for the historical Arthur was launched in earnest and since then eminent scholars have examined one candidate after another. No matter how thin the evidence, the conviction that sometime, somewhere there was a real, flesh-and-blood King Arthur remains as much an article of faith among those who love these tales today as it was among the chroniclers of the Middle Ages.

The artist Albrecht Dürer designed this colossal statue of King Arthur, cast in bronze by Peter Vischer for the tomb of the Holy Roman Emperor Maximilian I (1459–1519) at Innsbrück in Austria. The emperor wanted his monument to show the greatest monarchs of history: at the time no one doubted Arthur's entitlement to a place on this list. For extra authenticity his shield even bears the royal arms of England.

The historical "facts" that can be gleaned about Arthur from old chronicles, lives of saints and Welsh poems are meagre. The medieval Arthur probably represents a combination of several leaders, forged from the telling and retelling of many different stories over the centuries. If the legend of Arthur is stripped down to what is probably its most ancient and basic form, then the person Arthur-hunters are looking for was probably a commander or regional warlord who led horsemen against barbarian invaders of Britain in the decades before or after the Romans left Britain in AD410. He ruled either in the north or south of Britain and probably led a military expedition to the European mainland. This is just about everything we have to go on.

But there are other clues. The name Arthur is derived from Artorius, a Roman family name recorded in Britain: the earliest candidate for the historical King Arthur was Lucius Artorius Castus, a Roman prefect of the late second century ad. Artorius Castus used mounted nomads from the Eurasian steppes to help defend Hadrian's Wall in northern Britain against the Picts and the Caledonian tribes. He led some of these troops to the Continent to put down a rebellion in Armorica (Brittany), and his victory earned him the title dux ("duke", literally "leader"). This was one of the earliest titles ascribed to Arthur.

According to some legends, Arthur conquered Rome: this tale may derive from the exploits of Magnus Maximus, a Roman general based in Britain in the late fourth century AD. Magnus Maximus invaded Gaul with a substantial – largely British –

# The Round Table

Galahad comes to the Round Table; Italian, c.1390. The empty seat killed anyone not entitled to sit in it: its rightful occupant proved to be Galahad (see page 131).

*The Round Table symbolizes the brotherhood and unity of Arthur and his men. Its origin may be an old Celtic custom of warriors at feasts sitting in a circle around the champion.*

The table was said to have been created either by a Cornish carpenter for Arthur or by Merlin for Arthur's father, Uther. In the Middle Ages it symbolized equality at a time when society was governed by rigid feudal hierarchy: it had no head, preventing the knights from arguing over superiority. The table is depicted either as a solid disc (see page 103) or as a ring, as shown here. It is variously said to have seated anything from twelve to over sixteen hundred people. The idea that Arthur had twelve knights derives from the story of Jesus and the twelve disciples.

army and was proclaimed emperor of Rome in AD383 (see page 96). Another historical figure whose story may have become confused with Arthur's is Ambrosius Aurelianus (Emrys in Welsh). Ambrosius commanded pro-Roman troops in the south of Britain in the early fifth century and his main opponents, like Arthur's, were the incoming Saxons. In spite of his very Latin name, Ambrosius may well have been a Briton, a fact which gives a fascinating clue to the nature of Celtic British society at the end of Roman rule: the Romans probably left the province in the hands of a bilingual native aristocracy partly assimilated to Roman ways. Ambrosius may have been responsible for overseeing the resettlement of Celtic peoples from Britain to Brittany. He takes his place in the Arthurian legends as Merlin's father and Arthur's uncle.

Several other candidates for Arthur exist, but the most plausible is a figure known only as Riothamus, "Supreme King". During the reign of Leo I, emperor of the Eastern Roman Empire from AD457 to 474, Riothamus led British troops to the Continent, where he fought several battles. Betrayed by a certain Arvandus, the wounded Riothamus was last seen alive retreating toward the Burgundian town of Avallon, waiting for allies who failed to arrive in time. In the early Arthurian stories, Arthur was said to have been betrayed by a figure called Morvandus, who may be derived from Arvandus (in later legends it is Mordred). One of the most enduring elements in the medieval Arthurian legends is the failure of Lancelot to arrive with reinforcements before Arthur, mortally wounded, is taken to the mysterious Isle of Avalon.

# The Legendary Arthur

The tales of Arthur were rendered in every literary and artistic form during the Middle Ages. Chroniclers were sober in tone and strove to portray Arthur as a real king. Welsh, Breton and Scottish poets and French and Italian troubadours, however, encompassed humour, satire, horror, romance and fantasy. Storytellers adapted the legends to suit their public: Celts liked tales of magic, the French and Italians enjoyed stories of adultery and courtly love, and the Spanish and Germans preferred the pious legends of the Grail.

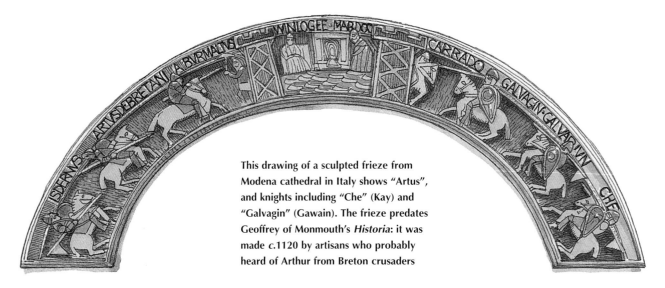

This drawing of a sculpted frieze from Modena cathedral in Italy shows "Artus", and knights including "Che" (Kay) and "Galvagin" (Gawain). The frieze predates Geoffrey of Monmouth's *Historia*: it was made *c.*1120 by artisans who probably heard of Arthur from Breton crusaders

In literary terms, the Arthurian craze began in the late 1130s with *Historia Regum Britanniae* ("The History of the Kings of Britain"), a Latin work by an Oxford scholar, Geoffrey of Monmouth. His book tells the "history" of Britain from its supposed foundation until the Anglo-Saxon conquest nearly two thousand years later. It is a vivid mixture of myth, legend and, occasionally, real history. Many of the characters are drawn from Celtic myth and legend, and the story of Arthur is the high point of the work. Tales about Arthur had already begun to circulate outside the Celtic lands, probably through contacts between the Normans and Welsh on the one hand and the Normans and Bretons on the other. Geoffrey's book was a runaway success and it was soon adapted and translated all over Europe.

The medieval Arthurian saga included most of the names found in the *Historia*: Arthur, Uther, Merlin, Guinevere, Mordred, Bedivere, Gawain, Kay and Yvain. Other familiar characters who are of Celtic origin but are not in Geoffrey's book include Tristan, Isolde and Mark, while Lancelot, Perceval, Bors and Galahad came out of French romances.

The developed saga began with Arthur's birth to King Uther of Britain and Igraine, wife of Gorlois, duke of Cornwall (see pages 110–11). The future king, half-brother to Morgan Le Fay and Morgawse of Orkney, was fostered by Ector and raised as brother to Kay. Tutored by Merlin, the twelve-year-old Arthur became king by drawing a sword from a stone (see page 111). King Bors and his brother King Ban, the father of Lancelot, helped Arthur to consolidate his kingdom. Later Arthur returned the favour by sending his knights to aid his allies in campaigns on the Continent. This young, brash Arthur is prominent in many of the legends. He is said to have taken several lovers – including Morgawse – but eventually married Guinevere.

Arthur founded the Round Table and summoned the best knights in the world to join him in the battle against evil. After the initial wars to unite his kingdom, he rarely entered combat. Rather, he presided over feasts and tournaments and judged disputes, leaving combat to his knights, notably Gawain and Lancelot. This worked well until the two champions fell out and plunged the realm into war. Most of the chronicles and romances portray Arthur as a wise and just monarch, God's elected, whose perfect kingdom nevertheless fell apart.

**The writer Walter Map presents the Vulgate Cycle to King Henry II of England; a 14th-century French illustration. This vast cycle, compiled by an unknown French author of the 13th century, encompasses all the stories of Arthur and the Grail, and was the most popular version of the Arthurian legend in the later Middle Ages. The cycle was for a long time wrongly attributed to Map.**

# Camelot

The French writer Chrétien de Troyes (c.1130–c.1190) first introduced the fortress-city of Camelot, which supplanted Geoffrey of Monmouth's Caerleon in Wales as Arthur's capital. Cadbury in Somerset and Winchester in Hampshire are among the various places suggested as the site of Camelot, but French romances locate it vaguely in the south of England. This imprecision may be deliberate: Camelot came to symbolize an ideal world in which all were equal before God. Medieval descriptions of the city resemble accounts of the heavenly Jerusalem.

**In this 14th-century illumination from Naples, an Arthur bedecked in Italian-style costume rides to Mass in a Camelot that boasts distinctly Neapolitan buildings.**

# ARTHURIAN SITES

**M**any of the places mentioned in the Arthurian legends are real and easily located on a modern map – among them the Welsh town of Caerleon-on-Usk, Arthur's capital according to Geoffrey of Monmouth's *History of the Kings of Britain*. As the saga developed, however, many of the central locations acquired names that made them much more difficult to identify: where, for instance, were Camelot, or Avalon, or the tomb of the "Once and Future King"? This lack of precision allowed countless local Arthurian traditions to flourish – enriching European folklore in places as far apart as Britain and Sicily.

*Above*: The so-called "Arthur's Tomb" at Carreg Coetan in Dyfed is one of many pre-Celtic sites linked with Arthur in local tradition. Arthur and his knights are said to sleep inside, waiting to awaken and serve their land again in its time of need.

*Above*: Tintagel in Cornwall is often said to be the real Camelot. The visible castle ruins are medieval.

*Above*: Bamburgh Castle in Northumberland, originally called Din Guayrdi by the Britons, is a candidate for Joyous Guard, Lancelot's castle and burial place in north Britain. Originally founded in the 7th century, Bamburgh was extensively rebuilt after 1066.

*Right*: Avallon in Burgundy may be the source of Arthur's Avalon. The legendary leader Riothamus, who may have been the prototype of Arthur, headed for Avallon after his last defeat (see page 105).

*Below*: Glastonbury Tor in Somerset once stood in wetlands, and some authors have identified it as the "Isle of Avalon". Glastonbury was also linked with the legends of the Holy Grail (see page 129). The tower on the Tor is all that remains of a medieval church dedicated to St Michael.

# The Magic of Merlin

Merlin, Arthur's chief adviser, is one of the most mysterious and fascinating figures in the Arthurian saga. The name Merlin is from Merlinus, a latinized version of his Welsh name, Myrddin. Some people have argued that Myrddin derives from a misinterpretation of the name of the Welsh town of Caerfyrddin (Carmarthen) as "Myrddin's Town" (the name actually comes from Welsh *caer*, "fortress", and its old British name Moridunon, "Sea Fort"). The modern public, familiar with Tennyson and films such as *Excalibur*, usually think of Merlin as a great wizard, but this tradition began only in the nineteenth century.

**Merlin (centre), Arthur (left) and the knight Meliadus are depicted in this Italian manuscript of *c*.1370. The image of the robed, grey-bearded sage may be derived from contemporary images of Old Testament prophets.**

Early medieval Welsh texts about Myrddin link him with the Caledonian Forest and depict him as a visionary driven insane by the horrors of war – drawing upon a Welsh version of the widespread "Wildman in the Woods" folk tradition. These stories, which sometimes also portray Merlin as a bard, have prompted the idea that he developed from memories of the druids of pagan Celtic times. In Geoffrey of Monmouth's *Historia* he is a Nostradamus-like seer who utters obscure prophecies in language largely derived from the Old Testament. Later the writer Robert de Boron (active *c*.1200) pushed him even further away from his wild Celtic origins and presented him as a clerically trained scholar and prophet. It is this Merlin who is featured most prominently in the Continental versions of the Arthurian legends.

Merlin was said to be the offspring of a nun and a devil who raped her. Blaise, the nun's confessor, foiled the demon's attempt to make the child into an antichrist, so Merlin was born with past knowledge and prophetic powers but with a good, instead of evil, heart. As a boy Merlin used these gifts to dictate the history of the Grail to Blaise.

He first came to the attention of King Vortigern of Britain, who may have been a real historical figure. Vortigern was trying to build a tower but the foundations kept moving. Merlin discovered the king's problem – two dragons fighting. Later, he served as an adviser to Arthur's father, King Uther of Britain, who succeeded Vortigern. Merlin's involvement in Arthur's life began when Uther spotted Igraine, the wife of Gorlois, duke of Cornwall, at a

Christmas feast. Merlin agreed to help Uther to sleep with her on condition that any issue from the illicit affair would be given to him. Merlin then transformed Uther and his henchmen into the likeness of the duke and his retainers. But while Uther lay with Igraine at Tintagel, Gorlois was killed in battle. Because of the unfortunate timing, it became common knowledge that Arthur had been conceived out of wedlock. Uther and Igraine then married, partly legitimizing the birth of the future king. Uther handed his son to Merlin, who gave him to the knight Ector to raise.

Years later, Merlin became Arthur's tutor and was on hand when the youngster drew the sword from the stone and became king. This famous episode was introduced by Robert de Boron in his *Merlin*. Uther died without an heir, because Arthur had been given to Merlin at birth. So Uther had a sword embedded in an anvil on top of a stone, and on the sword was the prophecy: "Whoever pulls this sword from this stone and anvil is the rightful-born king of all England." On Merlin's advice, after

Uther's death a tournament was called so that every knight could try to draw the sword. The twelve-year-old Arthur went to the tournament with Ector, not as a contender but as squire to Ector's son Kay. Arthur forgot to take Kay's sword, however, and was sent home to fetch it, but on the way he spotted the sword in the anvil. He decided to borrow the sword for Kay and – without noticing the words on it – pulled it out quite easily. Arthur repeated the feat before witnesses at Candlemas, Christmas and Easter. Finally, at Whitsun, he was crowned king.

Merlin became Arthur's adviser and when Arthur broke the first Excalibur, the sword drawn from the stone, Merlin helped to get a second one from the Lady of the Lake. Merlin's involvement in the legends came to an abrupt end when he fell in love with a fairy woman variously called Nimué, Niniane or Viviane, who came to be identified with the Lady of the Lake (see page 118). Annoyed at the prophet's unwanted attentions, Nimué sealed him up alive in a tree, a cave, or a tomb, depending on which version of the legend is followed.

In this Flemish illustration of *c.*1470, Merlin (left) explains to King Vortigern the meaning of the two dragons fighting beneath the ground on which Vortigern wants to build a tower. The red dragon, Merlin said, represented the Britons and the white the Saxons, whom Vortigern had invited to Britain as mercenaries. The Saxons, Merlin foretold, would overrun Britain just as the white dragon would defeat the red.

# Gawain and the Orkney Clan

Gawain, not Lancelot, was the original champion of the Round Table and he is numbered with Kay and Bedivere among Arthur's earliest companions in the Welsh romances, where he is sometimes called Gwalchmei. Through his mother, Morgawse, the half-sister of Arthur and Morgan Le Fay, he was Arthur's nephew. Gawain's stories contain more genuinely Celtic elements than those of any of his fellow knights. He is linked with Celtic sun symbolism – he grew stronger until noon, then weaker until nightfall – and some of his adventures seem to derive directly from the Irish tales of the hero Cuchulainn.

Gawain frees three captive ladies, after a French ivory casket: Gawain fights a lion; then he lies on a booby-trapped bed, but survives because he is too tired to remove his armour; finally the ladies await their rescue.

Tales of Gawain from England, Wales, Scotland, Germany and the Low Countries follow the Welsh romances and portray the warrior as the supreme example of chivalry and the champion of women. The French legends, following the lead of Chrétien de Troyes, use him primarily as a foil for Lancelot and depict him as a frivolous ladies' man – sometimes even as a murderer – who constantly fails to measure up to the French knight's physical prowess and superior, though flawed, morality. In most cases, however, Gawain emerges as an admirable figure, more accessible than many other Arthurian characters simply because he is so human.

Geoffrey of Monmouth recorded that Gawain and his family were from Norway. They became the rulers of the Orkney Islands through a slip of the pen: on a list of Arthur's knights, a copyist accidentally skipped a line between Gawain's father King Lot of Norway and the earl of Orkney. Lot was promptly assigned to Orkney, where he and his family remained in the medieval romances.

Gawain headed the clan after Lot was killed by his enemy Pellinore. With his brothers Agravain, Gaheris, Gareth and Mordred, Gawain helped Arthur to conquer Rome. After Lancelot joined the Round Table, Gawain befriended this foreign knight who supplanted him as Arthur's favourite. Gawain appears as a villain in the Grail Quest narratives, where he fails to attain the Christian ideal.

Gareth Beaumains ("Fair Hands"), the best-loved of Gawain's brothers, came to Camelot incognito and served as Kay's kitchen boy before volunteering to rescue a lady, Lyonesse, from a villain called Ironside. Before he left he revealed his identity to Lancelot, who knighted him. Gareth defeated Ironside and eventually married Lyonesse.

# Gawain and Dame Ragnell

*One of the most humorous Arthurian tales features an unlikely marriage between the courteous Gawain and Dame Ragnell, a Celtic-style hag of a type commonly referred to as a "Loathly Lady". Geoffrey Chaucer adapted the story for the* **Wife of Bath's Tale** *in his* **Canterbury Tales.**

One day a hideous hag came to Camelot in order to test the honour of Arthur's court. The hag challenged the king to engage in a riddle test. He would have one year to answer her riddle, but if he failed to do so he must grant her one wish. Arthur agreed and the hag asked her question: "What does a woman want most?" Arthur's knights spent the next year scouring every corner of his kingdom for the answer to the riddle, but without success. Finally, when the hag returned for her answer, Arthur admitted his failure and, true to his word, asked her to state her wish. "I ask for a husband," said the hag. Arthur felt honour-bound to marry her himself. His knights were horrified and Gawain stepped forward to offer himself as the hag's bridegroom in his uncle's place. Arthur readily agreed and Gawain and the hag were married. On his wedding night, Gawain approached his marriage bed with some reluctance – only to find that his wife had become a beautiful woman, Ragnell, instead of a hag. Ragnell explained to her husband that she was under a curse. "I can be beautiful either by night or by day but not both. The rest of the time I must appear as the hideous hag that you saw. I give you the choice whether to have me beautiful when we are alone at night or when we must face your friends and the whole court during the day." Gawain gave the matter considerable thought but simply could not make up his mind. In the end he declared, "You must do whatever you will!" Ragnell was delighted. "Your answer has broken the curse," she exclaimed joyfully, "and now I can remain beautiful all the time! For that was the solution to my riddle: what a woman wants most is her own way!"

**A 14th-century German embroidery of Gawain's adventures, as recounted in Wolfram von Eschenbach's *Parzival.* In this version of the story, Gawain overcomes several challenges to win the hand of the lady Orgeluse.**

# Gawain and the Green Knight

*In this tale, New Year is when the supernatural and natural worlds mingle, as on the Celtic feast of Samhain. The Green Knight may derive from Cernunnos, the god of abundance and forests, just as Morgan is related to the Irish goddess the Morrigan. A similar story occurs in the Ulster Cycle of Irish myth.*

At the New Year's feast, a giant Green Knight with a massive green axe charged into Arthur's hall on a green horse. He challenged any knight to decapitate him, on condition that he be allowed to return the stroke in a year and a day. Gawain took the axe and cut off the knight's head, whereupon the torso picked it up and departed. Almost a year later, Gawain set out for the appointed rendezvous at a place called the Green Chapel. He met a man in a forest who put him up, as the Green Chapel was nearby. The host proposed that he and Gawain exchange anything they receive each day and Gawain agreed. For three days the man went hunting, returning with much game for his guest. In the meantime, the man's wife tried to seduce Gawain and gave him one kiss on the first day, two on the second and three on the third, as well as a green belt that prevented its wearer's death. The embarrassed knight passed on the kisses to his host – but kept the belt. On the fourth day Gawain went to face the Green Knight, but the giant's axe merely scratched his neck. "That cut is for the belt," he said. "I am Bercilak, the knight of Morgan Le Fay, your aunt, who sought to test

**The Green Knight at court, from the only extant medieval manuscript of the story, written in England c.1475.**

the honour of the Round Table. You did well, but broke our pact by keeping the belt." Bercilak was none other than his host. Gawain returned home and Arthur ordered all his knights to wear green belts.

The villains of the clan were Agravain, Gaheris and, most notorious of all, Mordred. Agravain served as a companion to the vile Mordred. Spurred on by Mordred, Gaheris beheaded their mother Morgawse when all the brothers but Gareth surprised her in bed with Pellinore's son, Lamorak. Morgawse's murder tore the Orkney clan apart. Lancelot supported Gawain until the French knight accidentally killed Gareth while rescuing Arthur's queen, Guinevere, from burning at the stake. Gawain's unreasoning fury over his beloved brother's death led him to insist on fighting his friend Lancelot to the death. Gawain died from a head wound and was buried at Dover (although some versions claim that he was buried at Camelot).

In tales of Arthur's last battle, Gawain's ghost appeared to the king in a dream and warned him, in vain, not to fight Mordred until Lancelot arrived with reinforcements. In the end, Gawain's legend is the story of a noble but emotional warrior whose mindless, unchristian vengefulness contributed to the destruction of the Round Table.

# Lancelot

Lancelot, the pre-eminent knight of the Round Table, was a latecomer to Arthurian tradition. Introduced into the cycle by the authors of the medieval French romances, he was rivalled in popularity only by Tristan and Perceval. The families of both Lancelot and Perceval were said to be descended from the sister of Joseph of Arimathea, and all of the other Grail knights are related to them.

Lancelot was the son of King Ban and Queen Elaine of Benwick or Benoic in France, a kingdom variously identified with Bourges, Beaune or Bayonne. Lancelot was stolen from his mother by the Lady of the Lake shortly after his father died, and was raised in fairyland with the younger Bors and Lionel, the sons of his uncle Bors.

When he came of age, the Lady of the Lake equipped Lancelot with a horse, armour, sword, shield and several magic items, then sent him to slay one of her enemies. Lancelot accomplished the task with ease – and slew every other knight foolish enough to challenge him. He spent much of his time incognito, travelling as a nameless knight or disguised in armour that belonged to one of his Round Table comrades, such as Kay.

Lancelot's father, Ban, and his uncle, Bors, helped the young Arthur to consolidate his hold on Britain. This entitled Lancelot to share Arthur's rule

**The madness of Lancelot, an English woodcut of 1498. The knight's insanity, caused by his betrayal of Guinevere, is a recurring theme in the legends.**

115

# The Knight of the Cart

*Chrétien de Troyes's account of how Lancelot rescued Guinevere launched the knight's career as the most popular of Arthur's followers – and as the queen's adulterous lover.*

Lancelot in the cart, a 15th-century French illustration. Carts were used to haul people to prison or execution, so many passers-by assumed Lancelot to be a criminal.

The evil knight Meleagant abducted Guinevere and imprisoned her in his father's castle. Gawain went after them and encountered a knight forcing a dwarf to haul him in a cart. The knight was Lancelot, incognito, who had ridden his horse to death. That night, an innkeeper refused the knight a bed because he had breached the knightly code by not travelling on horseback.

The next day Gawain found the disgraced knight on the point of suicide. Gawain dissuaded him and they pressed on to the castle. Lancelot jousted with Meleagant and would have lost, but Guinevere recognized him as her lover and intervened to secure his victory. She was freed, but refused to see Lancelot, since he "would rather die of shame than rescue me!" Later, he redeemed himself from the disgrace of riding in the cart by beheading Meleagant.

over his lands, one of the many ways in which he was effectively an equal of the British king. He also won the right to marry Guinevere through combat before allowing Arthur to take her as his wife.

Many stories tell how, in the course of his adventures, Lancelot gained a wife by killing her father or husband. These early stories say nothing of Lancelot's adulterous love for Guinevere. In the Grail legends and the British tradition his wife is Elaine, the daughter of the Grail King, Pelles, and sister of Perceval in some tales. Elaine fell in love with Lancelot and by magic made him believe that she was Guinevere. The fruit of the liaison was a son, Galahad. Elaine later forced Lancelot to marry her. When Lancelot realized that he had betrayed Guinevere, he temporarily became insane, an episode that was frequently depicted in medieval art.

The Arthurian stories usually present Morgan Le Fay (see page 118) as the adversary of the Round Table. She often set out to kidnap Arthur's knights, and hounded Lancelot in particular. She took him prisoner several times, but he escaped with the aid of various damsels, hermits and even children.

Lancelot represented the medieval ideal of the consummate warrior and lover, but his adultery with Guinevere showed that he had human failings. He was one of the few members of the Round Table to survive Arthur's last battle at Camlann. According to later tradition, Lancelot won a castle, Dolorous Guard (sometimes identified with Bamburgh in Northumberland), which he renamed Joyous Guard. He allowed Tristan and Isolde to take refuge there, and when he died he was buried in the castle next to his friend, the knight Galehaut.

# Guinevere

All but invisible in the early tales of the Round Table, Arthur's queen rose to prominence in the courtly love romances of medieval France after she was paired with Lancelot in Chrétien de Troyes's *The Knight of the Cart*. Elsewhere Chrétien's plot was reversed and Lancelot won Guinevere as his wife by the secular right of combat before Arthur's marriage to her was sanctified by the Christian Church.

Geoffrey of Monmouth introduced Guinevere as a Roman woman, but her Welsh name, Gwenhyvar, comes from the Irish Finnabair, the daughter of the divine Queen Maeve of Connacht (see page 58). This links Guinevere with ancient Celtic goddesses of fertility and sovereignty, with whom a king had to mate in order to validate his own rule over his land. In spite of her fertility origins, Guinevere generally remains barren in English legends: an exception is the poem of *c.*1400 known as the *Alliterative Morte Arthure*, in which Mordred fathered two sons by her before destroying the Round Table. In Welsh and French stories Guinevere has at least one son.

Chrétien introduced the love affair between Guinevere and Lancelot, but the adulterous aspect of her character is in fact a Welsh contribution to her legends. In the story of Lanval, which was known in both France and Wales, an evil Guinevere tries to force Arthur to execute a poor knight, who has rejected her attempts to seduce him. Elsewhere Guinevere's character is less malevolent. In the Middle English *Awntyrs off Arthure* ("Adventures of Arthur"), the ghost of Guinevere's mother appears to the queen and Gawain, prophesying Arthur's imminent fall. Guinevere warns Arthur of impending disaster, but she is unable to prevent his doom.

In some French stories Guinevere commits suicide after learning that one of her sons has died. However, most tales relate that she entered a nunnery after Arthur's last battle at Camlann. These stories usually end with Lancelot claiming her body and burying her shortly before he also dies.

Lancelot and Guinevere share their first kiss in this French manuscript of *c.*1470. Lancelot's friend Galehaut looks on and Guinevere's ladies gossip nearby. Galehaut sheltered the pair when Morgan Le Fay tried to supplant the queen.

# Fairy Queens of the Round Table

Two of the most prominent women associated with the Round Table are the Lady of the Lake and Morgan Le Fay, both of whom share many traits with Celtic fairy-folk. In ancient Celtic tradition fairies were human-sized and tended to wear elaborate clothing and ride on white horses covered with silver bells. They were also inclined to abduct mortals – both children and adults – to live in the Otherworld. In Irish myth the fairies were sometimes identified with the divine race of the Tuatha De Danann.

In the Arthurian legends Morgan usually figures as Arthur's antagonist, while the Lady of the Lake generally supports the Round Table because of her affection for her foster-son, Lancelot. The Lady of the Lake originally bore no name, but in later stories she was identified variously as Viviane, Niniane and Nimué. She ruled a land which was entered through a lake. In early tales she reigned over both men and women, but later the water-fairy's court became an all-female realm. The Lady of the Lake rarely

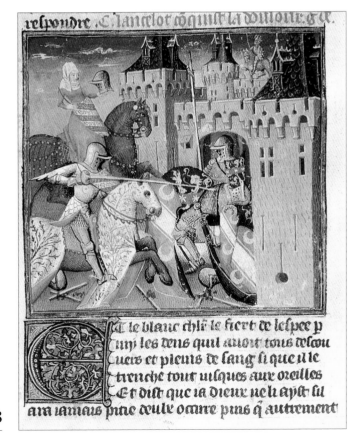

ventured forth into mortal lands, preferring to communicate with her protégé, Lancelot, and with Arthur's court through female messengers, as do most fairy queens in Breton legend.

Although Merlin was Arthur's original adviser in the legends, the Lady of the Lake assumed this role in later versions of the story, particularly after the introduction of Lancelot to the Round Table and after Merlin had been locked away. In numerous accounts she is identified as Merlin's lover, who imprisoned the sage in a cave, a tree or a tomb. Such stories suggest a strong association between the Lady of the Lake and death: certainly her realm, which was entered by crossing water, resembles the Celtic Otherworld, which the dead were said to enter by crossing the sea. Later traditions connected the Lady of the Lake with the mystic land of Avalon and designated her as one of the three queens who received the mortally wounded Arthur after his last battle (see page 133).

Stories of the Lady of the Lake only appeared in the British Arthurian tradition after the inclusion of Lancelot. It was said that she abducted the infant knight and his cousins, Lionel and Bors, and raised them as her foster children, schooling them in the arts of knighthood: in this she resembles the Irish female warrior-prophet Scathach, who trained the hero Cuchulainn. The Lady of the Lake was also renowned for equipping warriors, such as Lancelot

A 14th-century French illustration of Lancelot capturing the castle Dolorous Guard in northern Britain. The knight bears a new shield given to him by the Lady of the Lake, who is seen holding it on the left of the picture.

and Arthur himself, who received from her the famous sword Excalibur (known in the Welsh legends as Caledfwlch). She practised protective magic and created magical items to provide shelter and break spells. The Lady of the Lake also specialized in transforming people into their opposites, making cowards out of brave warriors and heroes out of cowards. She also used spells to promote peace, goodwill and congeniality.

Morgan Le Fay is the more completely Celtic of the two figures. The name Morgan is related to Morrigan, the name of the Irish war goddess (see page 25), and her supernatural nature is explicit from the outset in her clear designation as Le Fay – an Anglo-Norman title meaning simply "the Fairy". Her derivation from the formidable pagan war goddess may have led to a widespread reluctance to depict her in the Middle Ages – medieval images of Morgan Le Fay are surprisingly rare.

In the early legends Morgan bore a strong resemblance to the Lady of the Lake. According to Geoffrey of Monmouth, she was raised with her sisters on the Isle of Avalon, and became renowned for her shapeshifting, flying and magical healing skills. Her medical talents led to an early association between her and the dying Arthur, and she too was one of the queens who were said to have received him after his last battle at Camlann.

Morgan was the mother of Yvain or Owein, and Chrétien de Troyes cast her in the role of Arthur's half-sister and the aunt of Gawain and his brothers. Authors of the Arthurian romances came to use her as a foil for Lancelot, much in the same way that they used Gawain. As a result, Morgan's character suffered an unflattering transformation from that of a benevolent fairy queen to one of the chief Arthurian villains. In these later legends Morgan specializes in spells of deceit, and devotes much of her energy to concealing her true age, satisfying her ever-increasing lust and trying to destroy Arthur and his court. She regularly sought to test the honour of the Round Table, as in the story of Gawain and the Green Knight (see page 114). Morgan did not abduct children, but she regularly kidnapped Arthur's knights, particularly Lancelot,

In this 15th-century French illumination, Morgan Le Fay shows Arthur wall paintings done by Lancelot in captivity that reveal the adultery between the knight and Guinevere.

who passed his imprisonment decorating the walls of Morgan's castles with frescoes of his affair with Guinevere. The queen had earned Morgan's enmity by thwarting one of her love affairs. Morgan's activities then shifted from testing the honour of Arthur's court to attempting to reveal the affair between Lancelot and Guinevere. To this end Morgan directed a series of chastity tests at the ladies of Camelot, and her abductions of Lancelot were attempts to seduce him away from Guinevere. In some accounts Arthur learns of his wife's affair when Morgan shows him the paintings done by the captive Lancelot.

Sir Thomas Malory provided the most vicious portrait of Morgan Le Fay. According to his account, she plotted to kill the king and to this end sent Arthur an acid-lined cloak. She revealed to the knight Accolon that Arthur could never bleed to death as long as he wore the scabbard of his sword Excalibur. Accolon's subsequent theft of the scabbard nearly resulted in the king's demise.

# The Knight of the Lion

The knight Yvain, who is the equivalent of Owein in the Welsh Arthurian tradition, is best known from Chrétien de Troyes's masterpiece *Yvain*, or *Le Chevalier au Lion* ("The Knight of the Lion"). Chrétien's Yvain and the Welsh Owein possess many Celtic traits and have numerous features in common: each is said to be the son of the fairy woman Morgan Le Fay, and the two knights share a single storyline, in which the hero kills a foe, marries his widow, loses her love and eventually wins his way back into her favour.

**Yvain and his lion companion join forces to do battle against the giant Harpin de la Montagne in this late 13th-century illumination.**

Yet there are a number of differences between Chrétien's tale of courtly love and the Welsh legends of magical encounters in the Otherworld. It is possible that Chrétien's romance inspired the Welsh authors to use the character, since his work predates any of the Celtic Arthurian literature. The Welsh poets, however, may also have drawn on old British oral traditions about the historical Owein.

There are a number of characters called Yvain in Arthurian tradition, but Chrétien's hero is the most important. He is the heir to Rheged, a post-Roman kingdom in northwestern Britain that was ruled by his father, King Urien. Yvain and Urien are both historical figures: Yvain was derived from Owein, who succeeded his father Urien as king of Rheged sometime after Urien had defeated the Anglo-Saxons in battle c.AD593.

Although Owein was born much later than the likely period of a historical Arthur, the Celtic hero was presumably famous enough for medieval storytellers to incorporate his tale into the legends of the Round Table. The knight also played a minor role in the legends of the other Round Table figures, primarily as Gawain's cousin and a knight of the Orkney clan. He was particularly noted as one of the last people to be killed by the traitor Mordred

before the villainous renegade knight mortally wounded Arthur himself.

Chrétien relates that in the course of his adventures, Yvain mortally wounded Esclados, a knight who guarded a magic fountain in the enchanted forest of Broceliande in Brittany (now-adays called the forest of Paimpont). Yvain followed the dying knight to his castle. The portcullis fell on Yvain's horse and killed it, but Lunette, the maid of Esclados's widow Laudine, saved Yvain and presented him to her mistress. Yvain and Laudine married, then he rode for Camelot to seek knightly fame, promising to return within the year. He unintentionally missed the deadline, however, and Laudine rejected him. Like Lancelot in a similar story of inadvertent betrayal, Yvain became insane, and ran madly through a forest until he was healed by a magic ointment.

In the course of his attempt to regain Laudine's favour, Yvain saved a lion from a dragon. The lion became his companion in further adventures, hence his title the "Knight of the Lion". He also rescued the maid Lunette, who had been punished by Laudine after the knight had failed to return within the year. Eventually Yvain redeemed himself and regained Laudine's love.

Owein, the Welsh version of Yvain, owes much to Chrétien's romance, in spite of the old British historical origins of the character. *Owein*, or *The Lady of the Fountain*, a medieval Welsh romance that is sometimes attached to the *Mabinogion*, relates virtually the same adventures as those of Chrétien's knight, except that Owein is inspired to seek the castle near the fountain in the first place by a tale told by a fellow knight.

Owein's story also shows the influence of another of Chrétien's works, *Erec et Enide* (or possibly of its Welsh derivative, *Geraint and Enid*),

another courtly Arthurian romance where a knight foolishly loses a woman's love and is obliged to earn it back. This is also sometimes attached to the *Mabinogion*, as is another tale in which Owein features prominently, *The Dream of Rhonabwy* (see page 100). In the course of the story the knight plays a game with Arthur in a very Celtic, supernatural dreamworld after the battle of Camlann.

In this tale Owein's animal companions are ravens rather than a lion. This probably reflects the connection between Owein's mother, Morgan Le Fay, and the Morrigan. In Irish myth, ravens or crows were ominous birds, harbingers of death in battle. The war goddesses were often said to appear in their form, as when the goddess Badb landed on the shoulder of Cuchulainn to demonstrate that the hero was truly dead (see page 59).

## Lions

***The story of Yvain rescuing a lion from a dragon is a modified version of the fable of Androcles and the Lion, where the hero removed a thorn from a lion's paw and the lion became his friend.***

According to folk tradition, lions were born dead and came to life after three days: medieval clerics thus frequently used the lion to symbolize Jesus Christ. But a passage in the Psalms also links lions with the Devil. This dual symbolism accounts for strange allegorical tales such as the adventure in which Perceval met two lions, killing one and befriending the other – the first stood for the Devil, the second for Christ.

The Arthurian legends refer to three warriors who are known as the "Lions of Britain" – Tristan, Lancelot and Morgawse's lover, Lamorak, the son of King Pellinore. Tristan bore a lion rampant on his shield, possibly a reference to this nickname. Arthur also bore lions on his shield as symbols of his royalty. Often they are depicted as the three lions of England, which form part of the British royal coat of arms to this day.

***Above**: Lancelot fights the lions guarding the castle where Guinevere is held by Meleagant (see page 116); from a French manuscript of 1344.*

121

# Tristan and Isolde

The romance of Tristan and Isolde is the most popular of all the Arthurian legends. From courtly love and medieval burlesque to Wagner's opera and modern retellings, the love triangle of the knight, the queen and the king has enchanted audiences for centuries. Most of the surviving manuscript versions of this legend can be traced to a single work, *Tristan*, by the twelfth-century Anglo-Norman writer Thomas of Britain. His romance, which was composed before Tristan was incorporated into the Arthurian saga, may have been written for Eleanor of Aquitaine, the queen of King Henry II of England and one of the most remarkable figures of the age. The legend parallels the romance of Lancelot and Guinevere on a number of levels, and Sir Thomas Malory used the similarities between the stories to great effect in his *Le Morte d'Arthur*.

The character of Tristan may well be Pictish in origin: in Welsh legends he is called "Drustan son of Tallwch", who seems to be derived from a real person, Drust, the son of Talorc, an eighth-century king of the Picts. If so, this is the most significant contribution of this rather obscure people to Celtic and European literature. Welsh and Cornish storytellers probably linked Drust to Drustan, the son of Cunomorus, a historical ruler of Cornwall and Brittany mentioned on a stone at Castle Dore in Cornwall. Cunomorus has been identified with the King Mark of the Tristan story, whose name is Celtic (Merchyon in Welsh), rather than from the Latin Marcus, and means "horse". Isolde's name, Essyllt in Welsh, has been derived from an ancient British Adsiltia, which – like the English name Miranda – means "She Who Is Looked Upon". In the stories Isolde is Irish, and the basic love triangle plot may have been influenced by Irish elopement tales such as the stories of Deirdre and Naoise (see page 57) and Diarmaid and Grainne (see page 66).

The literary tradition of Tristan and Isolde presents Tristan as the son of the king and queen of Lyonesse, a country variously identified as Lothian in Scotland, Leonais in Brittany and a lost land beyond Cornwall. His mother, the sister of King Mark of Cornwall, died giving birth to him and her last request was that he be named "Child of Sorrow", Tristan – in the Middle Ages the name was

**Isolde, on her way to face trial by ordeal after being charged with adultery, puts a ring in a bowl held out by a beggar, who is actually her lover Tristan in disguise (see page 124).**

wrongly derived from the French word *triste*, "sad". The young Tristan journeyed from Lyonesse to Cornwall in the company of a tutor. He entered his uncle's court incognito and earned a reputation as a fine hunter and harpist.

Tristan won honours for himself when Cornwall was attacked by the Irish giant Marhault. The young champion revealed his identity to Mark as he was being knighted. Tristan's first mission for Mark was to secure a peace treaty with Ireland. He was successful in this task and later he brought

# Tristan in Ireland

*The triangle of Tristan, Isolde and Mark resembles that of Lancelot, Guinevere and Arthur. However, Lancelot and Guinevere's love arose spontaneously and followed the dictates of courtly love; Tristan and Isolde's was caused by an aphrodisiac and was both passionate and unapologetically adulterous.*

A giant Irish warrior, Marhault, sailed to King Mark's court at Tintagel and demanded that Cornwall pay tribute or be destroyed. Tristan, who had been serving at his uncle's court in disguise, killed the giant in single combat and was knighted for this deed. He revealed his identity at the knighthood ceremony. Mark was impressed by his young nephew and asked Tristan to go to Ireland to make peace and win him the hand of a beautiful Irish woman, Isolde. Tristan sailed to Ireland, where he found the court in mourning for Marhault's death. "My daughter's hand is at the disposal of whoever can slay the dragon that is ravaging my lands," the Irish king declared, then offered Tristan food, lodging and a bath. While

Tristan bathed, Isolde noticed the nick in the edge of Tristan's sword – it matched perfectly a piece of steel she had removed from her uncle's skull. She screamed "Murderer!" and attacked Tristan with his own sword. But the Irish king intervened: "You shall not kill a guest in my house!" Tristan slew the dragon and sailed for Cornwall with Isolde, whom he had claimed for Mark. Isolde's maid Brangwain brought a love potion on the voyage: any two people who

**Scenes from the life of Tristan, from a Sicilian quilt probably given as a wedding gift in 1395. At top left, Tristan kills Morolt (Marhault).**

drank it would fall in love forever. It was intended for Isolde and Mark, but Tristan and Isolde accidentally drank from it and fell completely and irrevocably in love. But Tristan, true to his knightly duty, handed Isolde to Mark when they landed at Tintagel. He watched in silent agony as his king married the Irish beauty.

An early 15th-century German ivory comb showing the famous "Tryst Beneath the Tree", which was depicted on domestic objects more than any other Arthurian scene.

back the beautiful Irish princess, Isolde, to be Mark's wife. On the boat from Ireland, Tristan and Isolde accidentally drank a love potion intended for Mark and Isolde, thinking it to be wine. They fell in love at once and persuaded Isolde's maid, Brangwain, to spend the wedding night with Mark so that he would think that his bride was still a virgin.

Try as they might, Tristan and Isolde could not stop loving each other and their affair continued. They met secretly in various places, in particular a certain orchard. Mark was alerted by his courtiers to one such assignation and hid in a tree to watch the lovers, but they spotted his reflection in a fountain and behaved with complete innocence. This episode, known as the "Tryst Beneath the Tree", was frequently depicted in the Middle Ages. Eventually, however, the affair was exposed. Isolde said that she would swear her innocence on red-hot iron in a trial by ordeal. On the way to the trial she put a ring in a bowl held out by a beggar – Tristan in disguise – and briefly touched his hand as she

did so. She duly passed the test by swearing that she had never touched any man save for her husband Mark and the beggar.

The lovers eloped and lived in the forest for a while, then Isolde returned to Mark, while Tristan was banished to Brittany. There, he met and married another woman, Isolde of the White Hands, but he never consummated the union. Prose versions of the tale tend to end with Mark murdering Tristan by stabbing him in the back as he played the harp for Isolde. Poetic versions favour an ending that appears to be directly lifted from the Classical story of the hero Theseus, who sailed on a mission to kill the monstrous Minotaur. Theseus promised his father that when his ship returned it would hoist a white sail if he had been successful, but a black sail if he had perished. In the event Theseus succeeded, but forgot to hoist a white sail. His grief-stricken father saw a black sail and killed himself in despair. In the Arthurian story, Tristan was dying in exile of poisoned wounds and sent word to Isolde to come to him in Brittany. If she was coming, the ship bearing her was to use white sails; if not, the sails were to be black. Isolde went at once to her lover, but the ship's captain forgot to hoist the white sails. Seeing the black sails, Tristan died of despair at the thought that Isolde no longer loved him, and Isolde died of grief at her dead lover's bedside. The two lovers were buried side by side. A vine grew from Tristan's heart, a rose from Isolde's, and the two bushes became intertwined: this motif was also very popular in medieval times.

Most tales include some version of the story in which Tristan stole Isolde from Mark. Often the couple are said to have found refuge at Lancelot's castle, Joyous Guard. In a late Welsh version of the story, Tristan and Isolde lived in a cave in the forest. Mark appealed to Arthur for help when none of the Cornish knights was prepared to fight Tristan. To settle the issue of who should have Isolde, Arthur declared that she should live with one man while all the leaves were on the trees, and with the other while all the leaves were off. The choice was to be made by Mark, the man married by the Christian rite. Mark opted to have Isolde when the leaves were off the trees because this would be wintertime, when he would most want to lie close to the warmth of a woman. But Isolde triumphantly reminded Mark of the existence of evergreens, which meant that in fact there was never a time when all the trees lost their leaves. As a result, Arthur gave Isolde to Tristan forever.

In another version, the lovers were sentenced to death, but Mark commuted Isolde's sentence and sent her to live among lepers. Tristan was imprisoned but managed to escape and rescue his lover.

The story of Tristan and Isolde appealed to audiences all over Europe, and the variations in the tales are countless. Scandinavian storytellers contributed an episode in which Tristan commissioned various statues to line a hall. Often, when the couple were apart, he went to embrace Isolde's statue. In some Danish ballads the lovers are an incestuous brother and sister, who in the end are poisoned by Isolde's mother. The Spanish and Portuguese gave Tristan and Isolde children, who rode off on new adventures after their parents' deaths.

This French illustration of *c.*1470 encapsulates the entire story of Tristan and Isolde. Aboard the white-sailed ship the lovers drink the love potion; at the end of the tale, the black-sailed ship sets off carrying their bodies from Brittany.

# *The Holy Grail*

Miracles happened regularly at Camelot, but none figured so prominently in Arthurian tradition as the manifestation of the Grail – the holiest of holy relics, and the object of a relentless quest by the Round Table knights. The Grail quest posed an almost unconquerable challenge for Arthur's knights. Most of them died on the quest and only one, Lancelot's cousin Bors, was successful both in reaching the Grail and returning to Camelot to tell the tale.

Although pagan elements abound in the Grail story, the legend was composed by clerics as a Christian allegory of, among other things, the soul's search for divine grace, represented by the Grail itself. Any pre-Christian aspects of the story have been recast and made to serve a Christian purpose. The legends of the Holy Grail became intricately linked to the popular cult of the Holy Blood, and many relics purporting to contain the blood of Jesus appeared all over medieval Europe.

The appeal of the image of the "Chalice at the Cross" may stem from a conversion tactic employed by early Christian missionaries. In order to convey

## The Chalice at the Cross

The most enduring image of the Grail in medieval times was that of the "Chalice at the Cross": the chalice used at the Last Supper, in which the blood of Christ was later caught as he hung on the cross. But the Grail has also been described as a deep dish, a blinding light, two vials of blood and a stone. Many Arthurian manuscripts depict the chalice alone at the cross, sometimes catching blood and water flowing from the wound in Christ's side. Such images are usually said to occur in visions granted to the Grail knights or to Arthur.

**The silver gilt Antioch Chalice, brought back from Syria by crusaders in 1101. It was hailed by many as the Chalice at the Cross, but it was actually made c.AD500.**

**During the Grail quest, the knights Gawain and Ector entered a graveyard called the "Perilous Cemetery". As this 14th-century French illustration shows, they were set upon by swords wielded by invisible knights.**

the sacred nature of the chalice in which wine was miraculously transformed into "the Blood of Christ" at holy communion, they may have compared it with various magical pagan vessels familiar to their audience. The communion chalice resembles to some extent the Celtic drinking horn employed in solemn chastity tests at Arthur's court. In these tests a woman or her husband had to drink from the cup without spilling. Only a select group of knights managed not to spill a drop and thus prove their moral purity. In some versions of the Grail story, the Fisher King heals a leprous monarch with the Grail. Some Celtic Arthurian legends feature cups, not identified as the Grail, that contain healing salves. The curative powers of these vessels figure prominently in such stories as the Welsh *Peredur*, a version of the Perceval legend in which women use a salve from a similar cup to heal men who have been injured in battle.

Another magical vessel was the cornucopia type of container that provided food and drink for all who sat at the table on which it appeared. Some scholars have argued that the Grail is derived from the magical Otherworld cauldrons of Celtic myth. The most famous examples are the cauldron of the Irish father-god, the Dagda, which could feed any number of people without becoming empty, and

the cauldron of Annwn, the Welsh Otherworld. The contents of this vessel boiled when it was breathed on by nine virgins, except in the presence of a coward. The *Mabinogion* story of Bran, who was once thought to be the original of Bron, the first Fisher King, features a "cauldron of rebirth" which restores dead warriors to life (see page 84).

Sometimes either an identified or anonymous figure appears with the chalice. Women bearing the chalice, who probably represent the Church or the Christian virtues, may have inspired the Grail maidens who appear in many Arthurian legends. The most frequent representation, of an angel or angels bearing the chalice, occurs in texts detailing the history of the Grail, in manifestations of the Grail at the Round Table and in the visions of Lancelot. Robert de Boron introduced the common scene of Joseph of Arimathea with the chalice at the cross.

The Grail legend was crafted by the medieval clergy and spread by monks and clerically-trained scribes. Ironically, the kind of monasticism usually

127

portrayed in the stories involves solitary hermits rather than communities, such as the Cistercians, who were responsible for the portrayal of the Grail as a blinding light instead of a cup. Almost every time that Lancelot suffered injury, nearby there happened to be a hermit's hut where he was able to recuperate. Other hermits offered prophecies to the questing knights. Perceval had a habit of running into hermits on high holy days, such as Good Friday, and receiving additional tasks to add to his quest for the Grail. These hermits tended to inhabit strange places, such as caves, pillars and trees.

The appearance of hermits – individuals seeking divine enlightenment – testifies to the great ecclesiastical interest in the Grail quest as a symbol of human spiritual development. In fact, the Grail stories were always most popular among clerical audiences. In an attempt to boost the wider appeal of these sacred legends, clerical authors drew upon well-known biblical stories and favourite folktales. However, the Grail legends were never as popular among secular audiences as other Arthurian tales, such as the stories of Tristan and Lancelot.

## The Early History of the Grail

Robert de Boron supplied much of the early history of the Grail in his *Joseph d'Arimathie* ("Joseph of Arimathea"). This was elaborated on in *Estoire del Saint Graal* ("History of the Holy Grail"), a romance of the thirteenth century which formed part of the huge French Arthurian compilation known as the Vulgate Cycle. In it, biblical and apocryphal tales are interwoven with material from the lives of saints and popular Arthurian romances to fabricate a history for the Grail. In these legends the Grail is usually the chalice used by Jesus and his disciples at the Last Supper. According to the story, Pontius Pilate gave the chalice to Joseph of Arimathea, who used it to collect the blood of Jesus, either at the Crucifixion or later at the Deposition, when Jesus'

**The figure of the resurrected Christ rises from the Grail chalice in this Flemish illustration of 1351. The scene shows Josephe, the son of Joseph of Arimathea, holding mass for the first Grail knights, with the four archangels in attendance.**

body was taken down from the cross. Following the Entombment, Joseph was imprisoned by the Jews and languished in his cell for several decades, sustained by manna from the Grail.

It was said that the Roman emperor Vespasian eventually freed Joseph, who converted the emperor to Christianity, then left with his kin on a missionary expedition through the lands of the Saracens. In Robert's version, some of Joseph's followers committed the sin of lechery, and Joseph built the Grail Table, which he modelled on the table of the Last Supper, to help him detect the offenders. Bron, or Hebron, Joseph's brother-in-law, caught a fish, which was served at the Grail Table. Duplicating one of Jesus's miracles, the fish fed all those who were innocent, and the sinners, who found that they were unable to approach the table, were subsequently banished. Because of this miracle Bron became known as the Fisher King and helped to lead the clan westwards, with the aid of two other clan members, Alain and Petrus. The successful Grail knights were all descended from these settlers. The Vulgate Cycle substituted Alain for Bron as the Fisher King and included the adventures of Josephe or Josephus, Joseph's son, who was said to have had a vision of the creation of the Grail and became the first Grail Keeper.

Joseph of Arimathea took his kin and the Grail to Britain, where the travellers converted the populace and where Alain, who followed Josephe as the Grail Keeper, installed the sacred vessel in Castle Corbenic. Among Joseph's followers in this endeavour were Mordrains, Nascien and Celidoine. According to several stories, Mordrains doubted the power of the Grail and was maimed as a result. He was cursed to remain so until cured of his injuries by one of the Grail knights, usually said to have been either Galahad or Perceval. Because of his wounds Mordrains was known as the Maimed King, a figure that some legends confuse with the Fisher King or Grail Keeper.

According to some accounts, Joseph finally settled at Glastonbury and founded the abbey there. One late tradition claims that he buried the Grail somewhere in the vicinity.

## Perceval

The legend of the Grail now moves forward to the time of Arthur and his knights. Merlin was said to have told the history of the Grail to the knights of the Round Table, and in most accounts Galahad was then responsible for instigating the quest to find the sacred object. The best known of the successful Grail knights is Perceval, one of only three – Perceval, Galahad and Bors – to reach the end of the quest and see the Grail. The stories of Perceval were the only Grail legends that ever became truly popular with secular audiences.

The early tales of this bumbling innocent, who was affectionately nicknamed the Perfect Fool by his fellow knights, were introduced into the Arthurian cycle by Chrétien de Troyes in his unfinished *Perceval* or *Conte del Graal* ("Story of the Grail"). The story, as derived from the principal sources, can be outlined as follows. Perceval's mother wanted him to know nothing of knighthood, since it had caused his father's death. She raised him in ignorance of his own royal background. As a young man, however, he chanced to see some knights and instantly wanted to join them. He journeyed to Arthur's court and became a knight of the Round Table.

When Perceval and the other knights rode out on the Grail Quest, Perceval's adventures took him to a barren wasteland, in which stood the Grail Castle. There he met the Fisher King, who was also the Grail Keeper. The king was cursed to suffer from a painful wound, often said to be in the groin, which would not heal until a predestined knight asked a certain question. When this happened, the fertility of the land would also return. While dining with the king, Perceval witnessed a mysterious procession in which maidens bore the Grail, branched candlesticks, a bleeding lance and other wonders, but he did not ask about these marvels because his mother had taught him that it was impolite to ask questions. The next day the castle was deserted. Later, a woman informed him that he should have asked the king a ritual question: "Whom does the Grail serve?" His failure meant the continued devastation of the land. Perceval was distraught, and wandered in the wilderness for five years, unaware of time, place or God. Finally he encountered a hermit who told him that the maimed king was in fact Perceval's uncle. The knight returned to the castle and this time asked the proper question. The answer is never actually specified, but the Grail Keeper was cured of his wound and allowed to die in peace, and the land flourished once more. Perceval succeeded him as Grail Keeper.

In Welsh sources Perceval is known as Peredur, the hero of a thirteenth-century romance of that name often attached to the *Mabinogion*. Peredur was confronted with a severed head instead of the Grail, and he later encountered a Celtic-style hag of a type traditionally known as a "Loathly Lady". In the *Didot-Perceval*, a French romance of *c*.1200, the hero heals the wounded king with the Grail, and in Malory's *Le Morte d'Arthur* he continues his adventures, only to die before returning to Camelot. The miracle of the barren land restored, made famous to modern audiences by T. S. Eliot's poem *The Waste Land*, may be a Breton contribution to the Arthurian legends. It appears to reflect the Celtic notion of the intimate relationship between the personal welfare of the ruler and the fertility of the land. Wolfram von Eschenbach's *Parzival* (*c*.1200), one of the greatest works of German literature, presents the Fisher King, Anfortas, as a Sinning King and the Grail as a stone guarded by the Knights Templar, a medieval order of chivalry. This version of the story, in which Perceval founds a dynasty of Grail Keepers, incorporates many tales that were brought back to Europe by Crusaders.

The story of Perceval inspired two masterpieces by Richard Wagner (1813–83), the operas *Parsifal* ("Perceval") and *Lohengrin*. Together with Wagner's *Tristan und Isolde*, these rank as the greatest German Arthurian works since the Middle Ages. The eponymous hero of *Lohengrin* is Perceval's son, who is certainly connected with an Otherworldly type of land. He first appears in a boat drawn by a white swan, and is known as the Swan Knight, which may reflect the Celtic association of these birds with the Otherworld. (The colour white,

This Italian illustration of *c*.1385 shows Perceval about to embark aboard a sacred white ship, which in some versions of the legend was said to carry him to the land of the Grail Castle.

which was favoured by the Celts to designate supernatural animals, figures prominently in the legends of Lohen-grin). Incidentally, this Arthurian opera includes a song for Lohengrin and his bride Elsa which has become one of the most popular pieces of wedding music of all time: "Treulich geführt", popularly known as "Here Comes the Bride".

## Galahad and the End of the Quest

The quest for the Grail related in the Vulgate Cycle of Arthurian legend is largely devoted to the story of Galahad, the son of Lancelot. His character was created by clerical writers in an unsuccessful attempt to combat the popularity of his famous father. Gala-had was said to have been conceived when the beautiful Elaine of Corbenic tricked Lancelot into believing that she was his lover, Queen Guinevere. A lifelong virgin, physically beautiful and morally superior to all of his fellow knights, Galahad proved to be a shining example of knighthood to which almost no one could aspire.

Galahad arrived at Arthur's court amid a flurry of miracles – including an adventure in which he, like Arthur, pulled a sword from a stone. He came to the Round Table and sat in the "Siege Perilous" or Perilous Seat, a place left empty as a reminder of Judas, the disciple who betrayed Jesus. It was reserved for an unknown knight who one day, it was said, would take his rightful place among Arthur's warriors. Anyone else who sat in the Siege Perilous – and several had tried – died at once. When Galahad sat down the knights were astonished to see that nothing happened to him, and were even more amazed when his name magically appeared on the back of the seat – he was the predestined knight. His relation Bors, Lancelot's cousin, recognized the young warrior and convinced Lancelot to knight the lad. After joining the other knights at the Round Table, Galahad had a vision of the Grail borne by angels or, in some versions, floating above the table. Everyone else saw only a blinding light. In the Irish version of this tale, Josephe, the first Grail Keeper and son of Joseph of Arimathea, returned to earth to display the holy relic for the chosen knight.

Galahad's vision prompted most of Arthur's knights to undertake the search for the holy relic. It was a quest on which many failed and from which most never returned. Gawain dropped out of the quest early on to pursue other adventures, most of them involving beautiful damsels in distress. Lancelot was also a waverer, but had several bouts of conscience, and his son Galahad inspired him to continue with the quest. However, Lancelot could not give up his love for Guinevere. He made it as far as the chapel door of the Grail Castle and just caught sight of the sacred vessel before being struck unconscious: because of his adultery with Guinevere he had been judged unworthy to have more than a brief glimpse of the Grail. When he came round, Lancelot was convinced that he was beyond redemption and finally abandoned the quest. He eventually returned to Camelot and resumed his affair with the queen.

In the end only Galahad, Perceval and Bors entered the Grail Castle, where they met either the Fisher King or, in other accounts, Josephe. They were judged worthy to approach the Grail and received holy communion at the Grail Table. In some variants Galahad, who managed to heal the maimed king during his quest, died and the Grail was taken back to Heaven by angels, since the vessel was too sacred to be left in a sinful world. Other versions of the story have Galahad ascending to heaven with the Grail.

In a number of accounts, Perceval also died after reaching the end of the journey, leaving Lancelot's cousin Bors as the only survivor of the Grail quest. Bors represents the common man, moderate, honourable and fair, whose down-to-earth decency renders him worthy of the Grail. In many respects he stands for the ordinary Christian, who according to the Church was as worthy of grace as the grandest hero. His very ordinariness probably explains why Bors is far less famous than many of his colleagues. Nevertheless, to him alone fell the task of returning to Camelot and relating the tale to the surviving knights of the Round Table.

**Galahad receives his sword and spurs in the ritual of knighthood, from a French manuscript of 1463. Lancelot, Galahad's father, conducted the ceremony on this occasion rather than King Arthur.**

# The Fall of Camelot

Adultery, betrayal, treason and civil war are interwoven in the tragic tale of Arthur's death. With the failure of so many of the knights to finish or even to return from the quest for the Grail, Arthur was all but defenceless when the evil Mordred arranged to catch Lancelot alone with Guinevere and exposed their affair. The events that followed led inevitably to the final battle at Camlann, and ultimately to Arthur's death at the hands of Mordred.

Guinevere's adultery caused a scandal which at a stroke destroyed the tranquillity of the kingdom. According to the law, the queen's affair was treason, and Arthur had no choice but to condemn her to be burnt at the stake. She was rescued from the flames by Lancelot, who accidentally killed Gawain's brother Gareth in the process. Gawain was enraged and persuaded Arthur to chase the fleeing lovers to the Continent, leaving Britain at Mordred's mercy. In the end Arthur and Lancelot settled their differences, and the king sent Guinevere back to Britain. Gawain found it harder to forgive Lancelot and eventually received a mortal wound from the French knight. Later, Arthur received word that

Mordred had abducted Guinevere and was spreading false reports of Arthur's death in order to claim the throne. The king returned to Britain to find his kingdom in chaos. He rescued Guinevere from Mordred, then granted her leave to enter a nunnery.

Arthur turned his attention to defeating the traitor. The opposing armies were drawn up on the field of Camlann, variously identified with a number of places, such as the river Camel in Cornwall and Birdoswald in Cumbria (which was called Camboglanna in Roman times). On the night before the battle, Gawain's ghost appeared to Arthur in a dream, warning the king to wait for Lancelot to

According to some accounts, Mordred attacked Arthur's troops in the Tower of London, as in this early 14th-century Flemish illustration.

# Arthur's Death

**In one famous story, Bedivere carried the dying king to the side of a lake, where Arthur told him to throw Excalibur into the water.**

Bedivere could not bring himself to sacrifice the sword, so he hid it and returned to the king. "What did you see?" Arthur asked. "Nothing," Bedivere replied. "Do not disobey me!" Arthur raged. Bedivere went off, but hid the weapon once more. Again the king grew angry, and this time the knight obeyed. As Excalibur hit the water, a woman's hand emerged, grasped the hilt, flourished the sword three times, then disappeared with it into the lake. Bedivere ran to tell the king, who sighed, "Now I can die in peace." Out of the mist appeared a barge bearing three queens. They placed Arthur in the vessel and sailed away from the shore. The queens may be derived from the Celtic triple goddess, whose three aspects – maiden, matron, crone – represented the span of life.

A 14th-century French illustration of the episode in which Excalibur is returned to the lake. Arthur sits mortally wounded as Bedivere throws the sword into the water, where a woman's hand seizes it.

arrive with reinforcements. To buy time, Arthur called a truce and met Mordred to parley. One of Arthur's knights was bitten by an adder and drew his sword to kill the snake. This baring of arms was in breach of the truce and the battle began before Lancelot and his troops were able to arrive.

Arthur slew Mordred in single combat but simultaneously received a mortal blow to the head. Different versions of the legends disagree on what happened after this. In some tales only Arthur and Bedivere survived Camlann. As Arthur lay dying beside a lake, Bedivere returned the king's sword, Excalibur, to the Lady of the Lake (see above). The king was then carried across the water to the mystic Isle of Avalon, which is generally thought to represent the Celtic Otherworld, the land of the dead. In other tales Arthur is said to have died in Cornwall at Tintagel, from where his body was carried to Glas-tonbury. Later, Lancelot buried Guinevere next

to her husband. Cornish legend claimed that Arthur became a bird, usually a raven – the bird associated with Celtic war goddesses – or else another bird associated with the Celtic land of the dead.

The most persistent tradition is that although Arthur "went away" after the battle of Camlann, he did not die. The Arthurian saga's most popular ending is a prophecy that he will return to lead his country in its time of greatest peril. Tales that describe his tomb usually include a Latin inscription: *Hic Iacet Arturus Rex Quondam Rexque Futurus* ("Here Lies Arthur, Once and Future King"). In some variants, Arthur lies sleeping with his knights in a cave or under a mountain, to be woken when he receives the new call to arms. All of these stories share a common conviction: that behind the tragic tale of Arthur's fall and the destruction of the Round Table lies a hope that the ideals of Camelot may live on.

133

# THE LEGACY OF THE CELTS

On the face of it, little remains of a distinctive culture that once spanned Europe from Ireland to Asia Minor. Most of the people who might nowadays regard themselves as "Celts" – the Welsh, Scots, Irish, Bretons, Manx and Cornish – do not even speak a Celtic language. And yet it would be impossible to erase the imprint left by the Celts on Europe. For a start, place-names constantly remind us of their presence. The ancient name for the Celts, the Galatae or Galatians, is recalled in Galicia in Spain, Galiti in Romania, Galatia in Turkey, and in the word "Gallic", from Gallia or Gaul, the old name for France.

Tribal names are even more numerous: Cornwall is named from the Cornovii, Devon from the Dumnonii, Cumbria from the Cymry or Welsh, Kent from the Cantii. In France, Paris and many other places have names of Gaulish origin. In England, the Anglo-Saxons mixed with the Britons for long enough to adopt many of their place-names. Most English rivers have Celtic names, such as the Tyne, Tees, Humber, Severn, Thames and the several Avons in western England (Avon is simply the British word for "river", Welsh *afon)*. Many English towns have names that are purely Celtic, like Dover and London, or Celtic in part, like Manchester.

About two hundred years after the fall of Rome, Celtic culture once more began to spread around Europe. The initial propagators were Irish missionaries, who roamed the Continent fearlessly, dispensing their brand of Christianity and founding monasteries from Iona to Italy. Irish books, such as those concerning the voyages of St Brendan, a sixth-century abbot, became highly popular.

By far the biggest Celtic contribution to med-ieval European culture, however, was the legend of King Arthur (see pages 103–33), whose appeal has endured to the present day. But for all the popularity of Arthur, it was a long time before Europe acknowledged its Celtic heritage. Historians were reluctant to believe that Celts were anything more than the barbarians described in Classical texts, and the rulers of France and England made every effort to stamp out the culture of their Celtic subjects. The tide changed in the late eighteenth century, largely owing to James Macpherson's bogus "translations" of Gaelic epics (see page 136). These famous forgeries evoked wild, brooding, elemental passions that caught the burgeoning Romantic mood in European art and writing. The Romantics created the flamboyant, heroic, shortbread-tin ideal of the Highlander. Ironically, this image was fashioned only after the ancient feuding clan culture of the Highlands had been destroyed in the wake of the battle of Culloden of 1746, which ended the last serious revolt by Gaelic Scotland. The novelist Sir Walter Scott (1771–1832) popularized the new image, and tartan became fashionable. English royalty, whose unpopularity in the Catholic Highlands had sparked uprisings in 1715 and 1745, fell in love with the place. Queen Victoria built a palace at Balmoral. Her German husband, Prince Albert, proudly sported a kilt on his visits there.

The excavations of Celtic sites at Hallstatt in Austria (from 1847) and at La Tène in Switzerland (from 1857) proved that the ancient Celts were worthy of the name "civilization". Sometimes the new enthusiasm for all things Celtic led people to claim that anything pre-Roman must be Celtic – for example Stonehenge (see page 41). Self-proclaimed "bards" erected stone circles in London and instituted the Gorsedd, a celebration of Welsh culture. More authentically, in 1880 the National Eisteddfod Association breathed new life into the Eisteddfod, a gathering held regularly since 1176 to glorify Welsh poetry and music through bardic contests.

The Celtic revival peaked between 1890 and 1914. In this period such figures as Lady Wilde and Lady Gregory scoured Ireland in their search for the

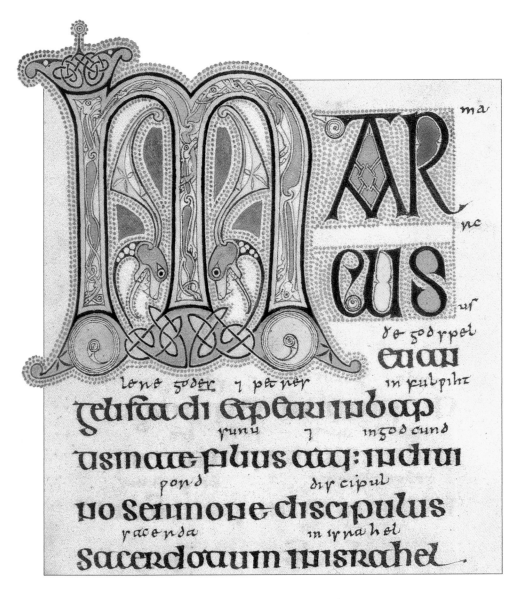

Under the influence of Irish churchmen and craftsmen, the English kingdom of Northumbria was one of Europe's great cultural centres in the 7th and 8th centuries AD. Celtic influence is clearly seen in the magnificent illuminated gospels (left) produced c.AD700 on the island of Lindisfarne off the coast of Northumberland by an Anglo-Saxon monk.

genuine oral tradition, which the Irish poet W. B. Yeats transformed into a relevant modern vernacular. In Ireland, cultural revivalism went hand in hand with political nationalism. The names "Fenian" and "Fianna" were adopted from myth by the supporters of Irish independence. This was won in 1921, although the Ulster Protestants insisted on remaining in the United Kingdom. Since 1945, nationalists have been active in Scotland, Wales and – most violently – Ulster. The fate of Northern Ireland is unclear, but the Scots and Welsh seem likely to achieve some form of home rule in the near future. Nationalist movements in Brittany and even in Cornwall have made little headway.

## The Language Question

For Celts in the modern world, language lies at the heart of what defines Celtic identity. It is the most obvious symbol of their distinctive culture (or, more accurately, cultures). Since Roman times, Celtic speech has given way to the languages of politically and economically more powerful nations. Sometimes economic necessity has overruled nationalist sentiment. In rural Ireland, the decline of Irish in the last century was at least partly the result of people encouraging their children to speak English so that they could work in England or America. Even in the twentieth century, children have suffered public humiliation for speaking Welsh, Scottish Gaelic and

135

# Scottish Myths and "Ossian Fever"

*The Gaels of Scotland are descended from Ulster migrants who originally settled in the Argyll region in the latter decades of the Roman Empire. The Irish newcomers took with them their Gaelic mythology, and also their name, the Scots – a term that was regularly used to mean "the Irish" until well into the Middle Ages. The Scots founded a powerful Gaelic kingdom which by AD900 had conquered the neighbouring kingdom of the Picts to occupy most of Britain north of Hadrian's Wall.*

Scottish myth and folklore is linked to that of Ireland in many ways – quite literally in the case of Fingal's Cave on Staffa in the Hebrides, a basalt outcrop which was said to mark the end of a road built by Finn from the Giant's Causeway in Ulster. As in Ireland, knolls were seen as entrances to an enchanted Otherworld. The fairy music that was said to emanate from these mounds formed a category of traditional Scottish song. Trees, particularly yews, were an important feature of the mythological topography. Animals too held significance – a deer on arable land, for example, was seen as an omen of war; swans were enchanted princesses. Shape-shifting features prominently in Scottish folklore, often in association with witches or hags, the greatest of whom lived in a corrie of perpetual snow on Ben Nevis. And like other Celtic communities, the Gaels of Scotland preserved a belief that one day a hero would return to restore them to their rightful position. When Prince Charles Edward Stuart, "Bonnie Prince Charlie", led the abortive uprising that

**Fingal's Cave on the isle of Staffa. The breathtakingly vast interior of the cave was the inspiration for the "Hebrides Overture" by the German composer Felix Mendelssohn (1809–47).**

ended at Culloden, he was widely seen as that deliverer.

Just as Geoffrey of Monmouth set Europe ablaze with stories of King Arthur (see page 104), it was a single author who aroused the world's interest in the myths of the Gaels. James Macpherson (1736–96), a Gaelic speaker, became convinced that the Gaels must have had a great

legendary bard whose long-lost works were waiting to be discovered in the remote Gaelic-speaking areas of Scotland. With the support of influential backers, Macpherson set off on a research tour. He found many poems and songs, some clearly based on old Celtic myths – but no bard. Macpherson was determined not to disappoint his backers, however – or to lose the fee they had promised. With some literary skill, he put together what he claimed were translations of epic poems by Ossian son of Fingal, a third-century warrior and bard. Ossian and Fingal were the names he gave to the Irish Oisin and Finn. The so-called "translations" that appeared from 1760 to 1765 were based partly on genuine Gaelic myth and legend, but sprang in the main from Macpherson's own imagination. *Ossian* was an instant hit, but suspicions were aroused when Macpherson proved unable to produce his "originals". Many people, including Dr Johnson, denounced *Ossian* as a hoax.

Yet Macpherson's disgrace did not stop "Ossian Fever" from sweeping Europe. Goethe, the greatest German writer of the age, praised Macpherson's works, and Napoleon carried them with him on campaign. Boys all over Europe, including two kings of Sweden, were named Oscar after Ossian's son. The Irish folklorist Lady Wilde named her son after Ossian's son *and* father – Oscar Fingal.

Breton at school. Nearly seventeen million people live in "Celtic" countries, but fewer than three million are native speakers of a Celtic language, and most of them speak English or French equally well. Very few Celts today have access to their magnificent literary and mythological heritage except in translation.

In the 1990s, however, it appears that all is not lost. Formerly hostile governments have relaxed their attitudes to Celtic cultural expression. In 1985 the Isle of Man voted unanimously to support "the preservation and promotion" of the Manx language, although the last native speaker had died on December 27, 1974. There are now many speakers of a revived Cornish language, whose previous last native speaker died in 1798. Welsh is doing particularly well. A quarter of the Welsh speak it as a mother tongue, but all Welsh schoolchildren, even in the largely anglicized south of Wales, now learn Welsh at school – an unimaginable state of affairs just a few decades ago. The Welsh-language television channel is the most highly subsidized TV station in the world. Scotland produces chart-topping pop groups who sing in Gaelic, although with 100,000 speakers the language itself has a precarious future; one minister on the Isle of Lewis recently remarked that it was now common to hear children in Gaelic-speaking areas talking English among themselves. In Ireland, too, nearly eighty years of heavy government promotion of the Irish language has done little to halt its decline. Only about 30,000 people in the far west of Ireland speak it as their everyday language, although almost everyone learns at least some Irish at school. Breton, the Celtic tongue with the least official encouragement, is in a parlous state indeed.

Only time will tell whether the belated official recognition of the Celtic languages has come too late. Some people have predicted that the Celtic tongues will cease to be used as an everyday medium by the year 2100. If this proves to be the case, it will be the first time in European history that a whole family of languages with a great literary tradition has become extinct. It remains to be seen whether the new "Europe of the Regions" – and the Celts themselves – will really allow this to happen.

**The decorative styles on this Anglo-Saxon gold clasp of c.AD625 from Sutton Hoo in Suffolk show that although their language died out in most of England, the Celts' cultural influence was more enduring.**

# Pronunciation Guide

The following guide to the pronunciation of Irish and Welsh covers only those sounds that differ significantly from how they might be pronounced in English. A simple guide to the pronunciation of individual names is also included in the index.

**Irish**
Words are usually stressed on the first syllable.

| | |
|---|---|
| **c** | as **k** in king, never as **s** |
| **bh** | as **v** in **vine** |
| **ch** | before or after **a**, **o** or **u**: as **ch** in Scottish **loch**; before or after **e** or **i**: as the "rough" **h** in **hue** (= **ch** in German **ich**) |
| **ll** | before or after **e** or **i**: as the **lli** in **million** (= Italian **gl**) |
| **mh** | as **v** in **vine** |
| **dh** | as **th** in **then** |
| **gh** | before or after **a**, **o** or **u**, it is a sound which does not exist in English (= **g** in Spanish **agua**); before or after **e** or **i**: as **y** in **yes** |
| **s** | before or after **a**, **o** or **u**: as **s** in **say** and **yes**, never as **s** in **wise**; before or after **e** or **i**: as **sh** in **shin** |
| **th** | as **th** in **thin** |
| **a** | as **a** in **mass** or **aw** in **pawn** |
| **ae, ao** | as **ay** in **say** (= French **é**) |
| **ai** | as **ee** in **see**, or **a** in **sat**, or **a** in **father**, or **aw** in **pawn**, or **i** in **sit** |
| **e, ea** | as **e** in **set** or **ay** in **say** (= French **é**) |

| | |
|---|---|
| **ei** | as **ay** in **say** (= French **é**) or **e** in **set** |
| **i** | as **i** in **sit** or **ee** in **see** |
| **ia, io** | as **ea** in **idea** |
| **oe** | as **oy** in **toy** |
| **oi** | as **o** in **top** or **aw** in **pawn** |
| **ui** | as **oo** in **boot** |

**Welsh**
Words are usually stressed on the penultimate syllable.

| | |
|---|---|
| **c** | as **k** in king, never as **s** |
| **ch** | as **ch** in Scottish **loch** |
| **dd** | as **th** in **then** |
| **f** | as **v** in **vine** |
| **ff** | as **f** in **fine** |
| **ll** | as **hl**, the **h** aspirated quite forcefully |
| **rh** | as **hr**, the **h** aspirated quite forcefully |
| **w** | as **w** in **wine** or as **oo** in **boot** |
| **ae, ei,** | |
| **eu** | as **i** in **fire** |
| **aw** | as **ow** in **town** |
| **oe** | as **oy** in **toy** |
| **u** | as **i** in **thin** or **ee** in **see** |
| **y** | as **u** in **fun**, or **i** in **thin**, or **ee** in **see** |

# Index

*Alternative versions of some names are included in round brackets. Where it will assist the reader, a rough guide to the pronunciation of Irish and Welsh names is included in square brackets after the relevant entry. A simple spelling system, based on Standard English, is used. Please note the following:*

*aa = a in father*
*aw = aw in hawk*
*ay = ay in say*
*ow = ow in cow*
*y = y in why or as y in yet*

*ch = the ch in check*
*CH = the ch in Scottish loch*
*GH = a sound not found in English. It is a bit like ch in loch, made further back in the mouth to produce a "gargling" sound like the g in Spanish agua*

*th = the th in then*
*TH = the th in thin.*

# Further Reading

**Compilations and Dictionaries**
Ellis, P B, *Dictionary of Celtic Mythology*. Constable, London, 1992.
Green, Miranda J, *Dictionary of Celtic Myth and Legend*. Thames and Hudson, London, 1992.
Jackson, K H, *A Celtic Miscellany*. Penguin, Harmondsworth, 1971.
Lacy, Norris J, et al., eds, *The New Arthurian Encyclopedia*. Garland Publishing, New York and London, 1991.

**Texts of Irish and Welsh Myths**
Gantz, Jeffrey, trans., *Early Irish Myths and Sagas*. Penguin, Harmondsworth, 1981.
Jones, Gwyn, and Thomas Jones, trans., *The Mabinogion*. J M Dent (Everyman), London, 1949, revised ed. 1993.
Kinsella, Thomas, trans., *The Táin* (The Cattle Raid of Cooley and other Ulster stories). Oxford University Press, Oxford, 1970.
Yeats, W B, *Fairy and Folk Tales of Ireland*. Colin Smythe, Gerrard's Cross, 1973.

**Texts of Arthurian Legends**
Boroff, Marie, trans., *Sir Gawain and the Green Knight*. W W Norton and Company, New York, 1967.
Cable, James A, trans., *The Death of King Arthur* (*Mort Artu*). Penguin, Harmondsworth, 1971.
Comfort, W W, trans., *Arthurian Romances* of Chrétien de Troyes. J M Dent (Everyman), London, 1963.
Cowan, Janet, ed., *Le Morte d'Arthur* by Sir Thomas Malory. Two vols, Penguin, Harmondsworth, 1969.
Hatto, A T, trans., *Parzival* by Wolfram von Eschenbach. Penguin, Harmondsworth, 1980.
Hatto, A T, trans., *Tristan und Isolde* by Gottfried von Strassburg. Penguin, Harmondsworth, 1960.
Thorpe, Lewis, trans., *The History of the Kings of Britain* by Geoffrey of Monmouth. Penguin, Harmondsworth, 1966.
Wilhelm, James J, and Laila Z Gross, eds., *The Romance of Arthur*, (the *Alliterative Morte Arthure*, *Culhwch and Olwen*; *Lancelot* and
      *Yvain* by Chrétien de Troyes; *Sir Gawain and the Green Knight*; romances of Merlin; extracts from Layamon, Wace and other
      works). Garland Publishing, London, 1984 (vol 1) and 1986 (vol 2).

**General Reference**
Ashe, Geoffrey, *King Arthur*. Thames and Hudson, London, 1990.
Ashe, Geoffrey, *The Quest for Arthur's Britain*. Pall Mall Press, London, 1985.
Barber, Richard, *King Arthur, Hero and Legend*. Boydell Press, Woodbridge, Suffolk, 1990.
Littleton, C Scott, and Linda A Malcor, *From Scythia to Camelot*. Garland Publishing, New York and London, 1994.
Loomis, R S, *Celtic Myth and Arthurian Romance*. Columbia University Press, New York, 1927.
MacCana, Proinsias, *Celtic Mythology*. Hamlyn, London, 1970.
Markale, Jean, *Women of the Celts*. Trans. A Mygind, C Hauch, and P Henry. Gordon and Cremonesi Publishers, London, 1975.
Piggott, Stuart, *The Druids*. Thames and Hudson, London, 1985.
Rees, Alwyn, and Brinley Rees, *Celtic Heritage*. Thames and Hudson, New York, 1961.
Weston, Jessie L, *The Quest of the Holy Grail*. Barnes and Noble, New York, 1964.

# Picture Credits